ADULT EDUCATION
POLICY AND PERFORMANCE

By

I. Ramabrahmam

Adult Education
Policy and Performance

ISBN : 978-81-212-0239-8

First Published 1988, reprint 2013 in India by
Gyan Publishing House
23, Main Ansari Road, Daryaganj,
New Delhi - 110002
Phones : 23282060, 23261060
Fax : (011) 23285914
E-mail: books@gyanbooks.com
website: gyanbooks.com

Printed at : Sagar Color Scan, New Delhi.

FOREWORD

I have great pleasure in writing this foreword to Dr. I. Ramabrahmam's book : *Adult Education* : *Policy & Performance*. He had been my student both during his M.A. studies in the Andhra University, Waltair and his Ph.D. work at the University of Hyderabad, Hyderabad. I must confess to an initial hesitation in writing a foreword to a work which at its thesis stage I supervised. Still, it is not difficult to overcome the hesitation in view of the hard work that the author has put in and the resulting good study that the volume has shaped itself into.

The contents of the study are not merely of interest, but of critical importance, to the students of Public Policy and Administration. The study deals with the implementation of public policy which in terms of the magnitude of its targeted clientele probably constitutes the most important one of its kind. For, the adult education policy, aims at uplifting hundreds of millions Indians from the 'educational poverty line' levels. The sheer magnitude of the targets exceeds any of the other purely economic poverty alleviation programmes.

Adult education programme can be regarded as a 'Grand Strategy' in the contemporary context of public policy theory when Health, Education and Welfare are not any longer regarded as spending-oriented policies but as investment strategies for the proper mobilisation of human resources. Perhaps it is apposite that the renaming of our Union Education Ministry as that of Human Resource Development should occur in the period precisely when adult eduation has received a boost in policy priorities.

If the policy itself commands our attention, the instrumentalities chosen for this—voluntary agencies afford equally worthwhile challenge to academic study. For, issues relating to the scope, extent and limits of the linkage between government organizations and voluntary agencies are subject of controversy in public administration. In terms of contemporary social administrative theory, voluntary organisations are not pliable supplicants to knock at the doors of the State for a small share in public service. The higher the public-spiritedness of the voluntary organisations, the more likely that they would project competing ideas and policies about public service and its priorities. The State, in particular, is likely to perceive the voluntary organisations as rival, if not positively dangerous, interlopers into the public domain. Given this adversary role perception between government and voluntary organisations, how does a high visibility policy implemented by voluntary organisations fare ? Further, there is the problem of the differentials in the motivational and organisational abilities and methodological perspectives of different voluntary agencies—involved in the implementation of adult education programmes. The book highlights some of these issues with competent analytical tools supported by adequate data base. The sample chosen is appropriately representative of the field of study.

The micro-level problems arising out of programmes involving millions of participants : problems like dropout rate, instructor motivation, physical infrastructure, are examined in detail and inferences helpful for appreciating the challenges at a wider level are drawn.

As a study in public policy evolution and as a study in organisational structures and inter-organisational relations this volume is a neat and competent exercise deserving good and generous reception from the public.

I compliment Dr. Ramabrahmam for his successful endeavours in bringing out his first book. I wish him many more such endeavours in the near future.

Dean RVR CHANDRASEKHARA RAO
School of Social Sciences
University of Hyderabad

PREFACE

The National Literacy Mission which was inaugurated by the Prime Minister on May 5, 1988 climaxes the efforts made to eovlve an administrative structure that could provide the necessary direction and correctives for the effective implementation of the new Adult Education Policy. It shares certain features with National Adult Education Programme (NAEP) launched in 1978, while differing from it in respect of the emphasis that it lays on such features as post literacy programmes. Further, it has the effect of imparting to adult education the status and character of a National Technology Mission. Furthermore, it facilitates the evaluation of such programmes in terms of their attainment of goals rather than their performance, besides evolving of new strategies for their effective implementation. It envisages its becoming a people's mission which is possible through the integration of the efforts of both Government and Voluntary agencies.

Considered in this perspective, the findings of the present study on the role of voluntary agencies in the implementation of National Adult Education Programme should prove enlightening in respect of the re-orientation of the NAEP to the attainment of the stipulated targets.

Divided into six chapters, this study analyses the reasons for considering adult education within the ambit of Public Policy and for including it as an important input in socio-economic development. It has the character of a pilot study, since it is based on field studies conducted in Andhra Pradesh which has the lowest literacy rate. It takes in its sweep the issues relating to learners, dropouts and potential learners whose responses have been collected through specially designed schedules and those accounting for the non-attainment of stipulated policy objectives. It is hoped that this study will help measure the performance of the National Adult Education Programme in relation to goals set by the policy on the eradication of illiteracy.

This study is based on my thesis submitted to Central University of Hyderabad for the award of the Ph.D. Degree. An inquiry of this nature is necessarily the result of what is gleaned, derived and learned from study and discussions with scholars, officials, respondents and various other key level functionaries, not all of whom can be individually thanked. However, I wish to acknowledge my debt of gratitude to those who helped me most in shaping my thesis. First among them is Prof RVR Chandrasekhara Rao, Dean, School of Social Sciences, University of Hyderabad, to whom I am deeply indebted for having supervised my research work and for having kindly agreed to write a foreword to the study. Indeed it is to his meticulous guidance that this study owes whatever merit it has. I may add here that I am solely responsible for mistakes if any.

I have had the privilege of meeting eminent scholars/ administrators like Prof A.K. Jalaluddin, former Director, Central Directorate of Adult Education, New Delhi and Joint Director, National Council of Educational Research and Training (NCERT) New Delhi and Prof. Moonis Raza, Vice-Chancellor, University of Delhi and former Director, National Institute of Educational Planning and Administration (NIEPA) New Delhi, who have generously given of their time to talk to me on various aspects of the national policy on adult education. I tender my grateful thanks to them.

I have benefited much from the discussions I had with Prof P.N. Masaldan, Prof Sisir Bhattacharaya, Professor & Head, Department of Political Science, University of Hyderabad, Prof. Haragopal, Dr. Rajen Harshe, Dr. Shanta Sinha, Dr. P. Manikyamba at various seminars in the department which helped me to clarify certain issues figuring in my thesis. My thanks are to them.

I thank Prof V.S. Prasad, Director (Academic), Prof K. K. Viswanadha Reddy, Director (Student Services), Prof Venkatachari, Prof T.V. Subba Rao, Director (Material Production), Prof V. Nagaraja Naidu, Registrar, Prof C. Subba Rao, Director (Evaluation) of A.P. University, Prof U.V.N. Charyulu, Director, Faculty of Human Resource Devpt. Dr. P. Durga Prasad, Dr. P. Leela Prasad, Dr. (Mrs.) Hemalata Prasad. Shri Kuruganti R. Sastri, Mr. E.V.S. Rao, Mr. S.N. Ambedkar, Mrs. Annamalai, Mr. Oomen John, belonging to different faculties, National Institute of Rural Development, Hyderabad, Mr. M. Kodanda Ram Reddi, Mr. K. Iliah, Dr. D. Satyanarayana, Dr. F. D. Vakiel of the Department of Political Science, Osmania University, Prof Y. Saraswathi Rao, Principal, Women's College, Osmania University, Prof K. Madhusudhan Reddi, Principal, College of Arts, Osmania University, for their encouragement and support at various stages of the study.

I am beholden to Shri T. Kameswara Rao, Lecturer in Economics, Government College, Pachipenta, Vizianagram District and Shri K.V.R. Subramanyam, Research Officer, Population Research Centre, Andhra University, Visakhapatnam for helping me to prepare statistical part of the study. I am grateful to Dr. B.S.R. Anjaneyulu for his constant encouragement.

I thankfully acknowledge the encouragement and support given by my colleagues and seniors in A.P. Open University, Central University of Hyderabad, Centre for Economic Social Studies, Hyderabad and Indira Gandhi National Open University and in particular to Mr. M. Chandrasekhar (Chandra), Mr. S. Vijayasekhar Reddi, Mr. C. Venkataiah, Dr. G. Sundershanam, Dr. K.S. Ramana, Mr. S. Sudhakara Reddi (CESS), Mr. P. Satyanaryana, Regional Director, IGNOU, Hyderabad. Prof. V. Bhaskara Rao, Department of Political Science, Kakatiya University, Warangal, Dr. M. Satyanarayana Rao (APOU). Dr. (Mrs.) Neela Jagannathan, Dy. Librarian, Indira Gandhi National Open University, New Delhi.

I thank the Project Officers, Supervisors, Instructors,

Officials and non-officials who have helped me in collecting statistical data and information. I wish to record my sense of gratitude to University of Hyderabad for awarding me with a fellowship without which I could not have completed my research work.

I hope to receive the UGC grant through Andhra Pradesh Open University towards the cost of the publication of the study for which I shall be grateful.

Finally, I thank Mr. Narayanaswamy of Andhra Open University, Shri P. Datta Raju, Shri Rajendra Singh, Shri R. Nagarajan (ASC), Shri A.S. Rama Rao and Shri D.R.K. Murthy for their valuable help and to Ms. Leela Rama Devi and Ms. Bharti for their neat typing and to M/s. Gian Publishing House, Delhi, for bringing out the work in an attractive format and that too in a record time.

I. RAMABRAHMAM

CONTENTS

1

Introduction

Adult Education, though of universal concern has acquired an urgency in Developing countries like India because of their attempts to step up their developmental efforts to match the aspirations of their people. In India various programmes and schemes of adult education have been formulated at the national and state levels which have become the subject of several studies. But few of them have focused on the Public Policies governing their implementation and fewer still, in fact hardly any, have examined the role of voluntary agencies in relation to other agencies engaged in carrying out schemes of adult education. The present study stands out by virtue of its being exclusively concerned with the examination of the relation between pubilic policy and voluntary agencies and its impact on their contribution to the promotion of adult education programmes.

Though Public Policy has been of interest to political scientists and philosphers since the earliest times, it has figured as an important subject of study only in the context of the investigation of the institution and structures of government and the resultant patterns of political behaviour. Again, it is only in recent times that the context of public policy has come to be studied for the purposes of examining the implications of various policies for the political system as such.

Public Policy can be viewed as dependent variable or as an independent variable depending on whether the influence of environmental forces and the characteristics of the political system on the content of Public Policy or the impact of Public Policy on them is to be studied. The study of Public Policy gains in significance, if considered in terms of its linkages with the environment and the political system, which would provide a frame of reference needed for spelling out their relational consequences. An analysis of Public Policy would be meaningful if it concerns itself as much with the content of policy as its determinants. It is not enough to analyse Public Policy on the basis of any systems theory because it will at best perspectivise the response of the political system to environmental demands or postulates, a kind of conversion process is generated helpful to the making of decisions leading to policy outputs as evidenced by the situational aspect of adult education.

Significantly, the concept of public policy has become virtually multi-dimensional because of the phenomenal expansion in meaning for that the two terms "Public" and "Pollcy" have 'undergone'. This is not surprising because the term public' has come to mean not only what the traditional conceptions of policy imply but also those traceable to non-formal institutions like political parties, pressure groups, media system which make up the scenario that the polity today presents. The advances in behavioural political science have facilitated the investigation of the stages or phases of public policy evolution which is in consonance with the new emphasis on the study of the various dimensions of the political processes as against the earlier emphasis on that of the institutional processes. Similarly, the word, 'policy' signifies any thing done in the pursuit of a preferred goal or goals, which includes the steps taken by the policy makers in targetting the goal as also the strategies formulated to achieve it.

A brief resume of contemporary definitions of public policy will bring out the implication of the foregoing explanation. Carl Friedrich, one of the earliest thinkers to define public policy in his book 'Man and His Government', defines it as"... a proposed course of action of a person, group, or government within a given environment providing obstacles and opportunities which the policy was proposed to utilise and overcome in an effort to reach a goal or realize an objective or a purpose."[1]

Friedrich believed that a policy is directed towards the accomplishment of some purpose or goal although it is not difficult at least in some policies to know the intention of the government. Richard Rose[2] defined public policy as 'a long series of more-or-less related activities' and their consequences for those concern rather than as a discrete decision. Here Rose is talking about policy in its composite sense of the term than policy as a particular programme of action. Further, Rose is also highlighting the distinction between the policy and a decision.

A very sweeping definition of Public Policy came from Robert Eyestone[3] who defined it as "the relationship of a government unit to its environment." It is so sweeping that one may find it all encompassing. Thomas R. Dye's[4] lucid description carries some precision with it. He stated that "Public Policy is whatever governments choose to do or not to do". Although he did not make a distinction between what government would decide and what they would actually do. Jamcs Anderson[5] in his book published in the seventies, defined Public Policy as "a purposive course of action followed by an actor or set of actors in dealing with a problem or matter of concern."

David Easton[6], one of the important behaviouralists defined Public Policy quite accurately. He recognised the role of various actors like elders, paramount chiefs, executives, legislators and judges, administrators, councillors, monarch and the like in the formulation of Public Policy.

Thns, the main implications of these definitions is that first, public policy is a purposive and goal oriented action ; sccond, it consists of courses of patterns of action ; third, policy is what government actually do in solving such problems like poverty, price rise and in promotion of people's welfare, and in protecting downtrodden people.

In all modern political systems public policy is implemented by a complex system of administrative agencies. These agencies perform most of the day-to-day work of the government and thus affect citizens most directly. It may not be necessary for policy analysts to be much concerned with public administration were it not for the fact that in all countries which were decolonized and became independent, the bureaucracy occupies the most important place in policy formulation and implementation.[7] The traditional notion that politics and administration are two distinct spheres of activity is no longer accepted. It is true that well known authorities like Goodnow[8] made a good distinction between Politics and Public administration. Politics, according to Frank Goodnow, is concerned with the formulation of the will of the State, value judgements and determining what government should] or should not do and it is to be handled by the 'political' branches of government, i.e. the legislature and the executive. Administration on the other hand in his view is concerned with the implementation of the will of the State and the carrying out more or less automatically of the decisions of the political branches. Administration deals with questions of fact, 'what is' rather that 'what ought to be,' and consequently can focus on the most efficient means of implementing policy. But his facile distinction that preoccupation of political science is with normative policy matters and that of administration with mundane matters of how to implement a given policy is untenable.

Modern administrative agencies often operate under broad and ambiguous rules and regulations which leave them with much discretion to decide what should or should not be done. Owing to lack of time, interest, information and expertise on the part of the legislatures to some extent the administrative process has become an extension of legislative process and administrators find themselves immersed in politics in modern political system.

While administrative agencies are the primary implementors of Public Policy, there are several other agencies/actors involved in the process of implementation of a policy.

It may be interesting to note here that the contemporary studies in public administration now take under their scope areas that were in the past regarded as alien to political science or public administration. As the variety of state intervention through public policy increases, the nature and scope of the public administration studies increases. Educational policy in particular is a good example. From an orthodox point of view, education is a subject reserved for educationists. But, from a contemporary policy point of view, given the policy administrative components that together are intended to promote education, the study of education and its related policy has come to occupy the attention of the students of public administration too.

Further, it will be noticed that within the area of educational policy, the sub-area of adult education is even more challenging and germane to public policy studies. For, essentially, policies like adult education are different from other policies like policy on imports and exports, industrial development, prohibition, anti-corruption etc. In all democratic countries, the governments can legislate on any of these policies and make people comply with them. Governments can even use their authority to implement these policies. But qualitative policies like adult education very much depend on factors like motivation, persuasion etc. Coercive devices are less of a guarantee in the realization of such a qualitative policy as adult education.

The pre as well as post independent India saw many an experimentation in the policy on adult education. In post independent India, many ventures were made in the field of education. While some of these programmes failed because of bureaucratization, others failed due to lack of a proper policy will. The policy on adult education because of its qualitative nature also gives rise to some fundamental questions regarding the strategies of implementation of public policies. Third World countries are now gradually realising that some policies require different strategies of implementation. The main reason for this new thinking is the inadequacy of existing institutional arrangement in these countries. Theoreticains of public policy have been posing this question for quite some time. Should every policy, be it growth oriented, production oriented, or quality oriented be entrusted to the bureaucracy ? There is already a popular notion that only through gradual de-bureaucratization can goals of certain policies be realised. This is because bureaucracy is growing dysfunctional at least in some areas of public policy. For example, in a crucial area like Community Development which involved attitudinal and motivational change, bureaucratization of the entire programme failed to deliver the goods. This is not to say that bureaucratization is necessarily bad. The point is that the notion that bureaucracy is a panacea for the establishment of a welfare state (a notion that became very common in the post war democratic world) is now under critical evaluation and this is not only from the conventional quarters like Hayek[9] and Von Mises[10] who were against the very idea of interventionist state.

Since the fifties new thrusts or strategies of developmental policy have enormously increased the role of bureaucracy in India which has adversely affected its efficiency. For instance, the Community Development Programme has not succeeded to the extent desired because of its heavy bureaucratized nature. In the sixties, the Panchayat Raj institutions failed because of lack of political will, again they went to bureaucracy, in the seventies special agencie like Drought Prone Area Programme (D P A P), Small Farmers Development Agency (S F D A)were created with heavy bureaucratized structures, and now in the eighties an intergrated approach has came into existence dominated again by bureaucracy.

Milton Esman[11] an eminent authority on rural development while analysing the processes of development in the Third World countries identified four instruments of action which facilitate nation building and socio-economic development. They are (1) political organization, (2) administrative system, (3) associational interest groups and the (4) mass media. The author's veiws on associational/voluntary groups deserve a mention here. Discussing the importance of the voluntary agencies, he wrote that "deliberate social change may be greatly facilitated by community organization. In the performance of many service and control functions, governments cannot deal effectively with unorganized individuals. It is thus important that the community be organized in order to relate effectively to the administrative institutions performing services associated with nation building and development programmes".[12]

Esman saw three advantages in associating the voluntary agencies with the implementation of public policies : (1) a sense of solidarity, (2) opportunity to interact with agencies of development/government and (3) participatian in decision-making.[13]

The developing countries are passing through a critical phase as there the administrative systems are touching new depths of inefficiency owing to increasing demands on it. Voluntary agencies with their flexible system, informality and commitment would channelise the energies of the people towards a positive goal. One more advantage which the voluntary agencies have is their inner motivation. It is generally believed that voluntary agencics are free from colonial bureaucratic legacy like bureaucratic indifference. Their indigenous roots, it was believed, would result in humanizing the system. Some feel that the state can assign them a complementary role in the implementation of public policies. The earlier experience of over-bureaucratization of developmental agencies/institutions and the continuing gap between promise and performance of state machinery also led to a scarch for alternatives. Voluntarism is increasingly being shown as an emerging trend.

It has already been mentioned how certain types of public policy, particularly those involving critical changes in human attitudes and values are less suited to be accomplished by bureaucracies. That is why in the theory of development administration the role of bureaucracy frequently comes in for critical evaluation.

Educational policy constitutes one of the prime parts of a development package seeking to affect attitudinal change in societies. Primary and adult education in general are regarded as the key factors in initiating that attitudinal change. And it is in this field of primary and adult education that the role of non-bureaucratic agencies as in-puts into the policy process is highlighted.

In India, voluntary agencies have long been involved in what is generally called social work. As the role of formal education has come to be accepted as an imperative for creating the necessary value changes to facilitate development, voluntary agencies have become an important component of the public policy process. That is why the role of these agencis in the implementation of public policy becomes germane to studies in public policy.

While before independence, Voluntary Agencies were generally known to be involved in the area of adult education, adult education itself did not form part of an official public policy. An interesting point can be raised here. Even in the evolution of the concept of the Welfare State, quite a range of 'policies' do ultimately emerge as part of the package of public policy. But some of these or some aspects of these might take some time in projecting themselves as public policy. In other words, a certain item may have become an obvious candidate for public policy, but its contemporary obviousness should not obscure the fact that in earlier times it was not so obviously regarded. The area of adult education is a good instance of this. Even earlier, education had been recognized as part of governmental concern and thus as part of public policy. But within this, adult education has not been so recognized even though governments may have recognized this to be an activity complementing their own commitment to the promotion of formal education. What happened after independence is that even adult education finds incorporation into the range of professed public policy. Along with it, the role of voluntary agencies also became an integral aspect of public policy. It would now be necessary to discuss the evolution of the item of adult education as part of the public policy process in India.

Evolution of policy on Adult Education

Before independence adult education did not figure prominently in the agenda of the public policy. The work of adult education was taken by private (voluntary) organizations. The various social reform movements in the nineteenth century and the rise of Indian nationalism helped greatly in increasing the necessity for literacy. In rousing the consciousness of the people, the social reform movements simultaneously also led to an increase in the demand for education. This period also marks the beginning of the importance of regional languages.

As early as 1848, the Andhra Evangelical Church, Guntur (about 400 km South of Hyderabad, Capital of Andhra Pradesh) had literacy as one of its programmes. The movement for Home Rule further encouraged people to take interest in adult education work. Various organizations like the Servants of India Society (1905), the Seva Sadan (1908), Mahila Samaj (1910), the Socialist League (1911) were instrumental in educating illiterate adults.[14]

The provincial governments in the latter half of the nineteenth century and in the beginning of the twentieth century organized in big towns a number of schools with the specific purpose of recruiting people with some knowledge in English.

It is voluntary agencies which mostly took up the challenge of illiteracy, thus exhibiting a better awareness of the bane of illiteracy to human progress. Much of the ground work in this area was done by the voluntary agencies before the colonial government could even give a thought to it.

The entry of Mahatma Gandhi in the national movement in 1920's gave a new fillip to adult education movement. Gandhi with his unique technique of combining political activity with constructive work directed the nation's creative energy, towards the goal of rebuilding India. The switch over from political activity to constructive activity made the people pay increasing attention to the problems of adult education. Though Gandhi may not be accepted as an educationist as we understand the word today, his views are worth a reference here. According to him "education does not mean a knowledge of letters, that is, ability to read and write, as it is ordinarily understood to be".[15] Literacy, according to him is "only one of the means, a sort of on instrument, for acquiring education". Further he noted that "education, that helps to build up sound character and promotes self-development, is true education."[16] By education he meant "an alround drawing out of the best, in child and man, body, mind and spirit".[17]

Basic education, is yet another expression of Indian origin, of which the author was no less than Gandhi.[18] Aimed at reforming the book-centred education, the main features of this system include (1) instruction through the mother tongue, (2) interrelating the education with social and physical environment of the students (3) development of creative aptitude of the learner through useful craft or manual work (in other words, imparting of such knowledge as can be correlated to some basic craft), and (4) treating the school as a productive unit.

The views of Gandhi on adult education are very much relevant even today. In one of his articles he said "my adult education means true political education of the adult by word of mouth...side by side with the education by the mouth will be the literacy education".[19] Thus the views of Gandhi mentioned above reveal his perception of the role of education, the new concept of basic education as well as his idea on adult education. No doubt these ideas have, to some extent, influenced our national leaders and policies.

The Independence of India in 1947 aroused great hopes about many things and especially about radical reconstruction of Indian education. The Indian national leadership had always expressed great faith in the use of education for modernization and development and had shown deep and continuing interest in the radical transformation of colonial educational system built up by British adminisrators As early as 1906, the Indian National Congress adopted a resolution on National Education which said that the time had come "for the people all over the country earnestly to take up the question of national education for both boys and girls and organize a system of education, literary, scientific and technical suited to the requirements of the country on national lines under national control and directed towards the realisation of national destiny".[20] Of the areas which needed immediate attention, adult education was identified as one such area. Later Gandhi's ideas on education, basic education and adult education were widely quoted, and the benefits of literacy were also discussed and debated. Particularly Gandhi's call for liquidation of illiteracy which he termed as India's sin and shame had roused the conscience of the popular national leadership at that time.

In fact, in the first educational ministers' conference of free India, Nehru said that "whenever conferences were called to form a plan for education in India, as a rule, it was to maintain the existing system with slight modifications. This must not happen now. Great changes have taken place in the country and education system must also be in keeping with them. The entire basis of education must be revolutionized".[21]

However, for various reasons the promised revolution in education did not come about. It is not that educational reforms were not attempted. In fact many good and useful policies were adopted and programmes introduced. However, the events that took place in the educational field in India are rather discouraging.

While acceptance of adult education as an item of the package of public policy of Education was hailed by some as revolutionary, others have even termed them as evolutionary and reformist policies not taken with the clear intention to achieve the goal of liquidation of illiteracy.

An examination of the policies pursued by the government in the field of adult education reveals that there is a considerable amount of discrepancy between theory and practice and promise and performance. The repeated assertions of the government about their commitment to adult education was not properly reflected in the five year plans in terms of allocation of resources. The following table contains the allocations made to different sectors in education up to the fifth five year plan.

There are also instances where funds meant for adult education have been diverted to other sections on various pretexts. The issue of adult education as such also suffered to some extent because of absence of vocal support within and outside Parliament.

The above table is self-explanatory. While there has been a gradual increase in expenditure on elementary, secondary, technical and higher education, adult education has hardly received any attention. In fact, in the first three plans there was actually a decline on expenditure on adult education.

On the other hand, we notice an increase in the number of adult illiterates above the age of 15 years from 1951 to 1971. The following table gives the figures relating to increase in the number of adult illiterates.

TABLE 1

Financial Allocation to Different Educational Sectors (1951-78)*

(in millions of Rs.)

Sectors of Education	I	II	III	IV	V
Higher Education	140 (9.7)	480 (19.4)	870 (16.8)	6352 (13.9)	14682 (15.2)
Technical Education	200 (13.9)	490 (19.8)	1250 (24.1)	2619 (5.8)	4434 (4.6)
Secondary Education	200 (13.9)	510 (20.7)	1030 (19.9)	14871 (32.6)	31277 (32.4)
Elementary Education	850 (59.0)	950 (38.5)	3010 (38.8)	21681 (47.6)	45819 (47.5)
Adult Education	50 (3.5)	40 (1.6)	20 (0.4)	59 (0.1)	326 (0.3)
Total	1440 (100.00)	2470 (100.00)	5180 (100.00)	45582 (100.00)	96538 (100.00)

*Source : Report of the Review Committee on National Education Programme 1982, p. 9,

TABLE 2

Adult Illiterates in the age group of 15 and above.*

Year	Total Population	15 and above	Illiterate Male	Population Female
1951	2150.17	1735.73 (80.74)	784.93	950.80
1961	2528.54	1870.02 (72.24)	782.28	1087.74
1971	3178.25	2095.11 (65.92)	863.80	1231.31

*Report of the *Committee on Adult Education for Women*, Govt. of India, Ministry of Education and Social Welfare, New Delhi 1978, p. 5.

The table reveals that although there is a gradual reduction in the percentage of illiterates during the years 1951 to 1971 yet the progress is far from satisfactory, considering the situation in other developing countries. The argument that the total number of illiterates is increasing owing to increase in population only confirms the view that efforts are not made in the shape of proper policies to tackle the problem of illiteracy among adults.

It would be profitable here to go into the reasons for the existing state of education policy in general and the policy on adult education in particular.

Two important reasons were cited by J.P. Naik,[22] an eminent educationist. for the slow progress in the field of education in general and adult education in particular. They are (1) the political decisions and (2) the educational decisions. As education is a sub-system of the social system, it cannot be revolutionaized unless a social revolution takes places first or unless a simultaneous revolution takes place.

In this connection an important point about the casual connection between changes in the educational system on the one hand and changes in the social system on the other needs to be highlighted. Conventionally, people speak of changes in the educational system leading to socio-economic change and in this context, talk of even revolutionary changes is not uncommon. There are others who say that the conventional formulation puts the cart before the horse. To these, education being a function of society and an educational system being a sub-system of the social system, revolution in education can be thought of only as a consequence of (or at best contemporaneous with) a revolution in the social structure itself.

The basic difficulty with the Indian Education Policy seems to be twofold : First, education is regarded as the instrument for social change and some critics question the casual implications of this equation. They believe that unless society itself is altered by a package of strategies, the nature of the educational system cannot itself be effectively changed. This is no doubt a fundamentalist argument. It must be admitted that a policy of trying to change a social system through education is not in itself invalid howsoever conventional and old fashioned it may appear. The other aspect of the lacunae in Indian educational policy is that there has been a manifest failure in appreciating the magnitude of the change that is to be brought about in educational policy, granting that through changes in educational policy a transformation in the social system can be brought about. For instance, the vastness and magnitude of illiteracy in India never seems to have been fully grasped by policy makers, even when they were articulating loudly the strategies of adult education. The formulation of policy was based on a very casual incrementalist approach—casual incrementalism amounting to ad-hocism. Hence all the educational decisions taken were based on the concept of stability with change and in an evolutionary and reformist perspective.

It was argued that the partition of the country had created a delicate situation in which the very survival of the country was at stake. It was felt desirable to postpone all decisions to a later date and to concentrate all efforts to consolidation of freedom and nation building. Of course, none of the issues was re-opened like Mahatma Gandhi's call for disbanding Congress ; his model for development which he mentioned in Hindu Swaraj was ignored. On the contrary, western model of development based on science and technology, modernization of agriculture, heavy industralization were given priority.

In the adminisrration too radical reform were not attempted to suit our system and only a change in nomenclature from Indian Civil Service to Indian Administrative Service was made. According to some, the reason was that these decisions were taken in the interests of ruling groups which came to power in 1949. The westernized class created by the Brititish developed a national pride. Some writers called this change in India from western to the westernized. These classes have determined to continue to rule with such attention to the welfare of the poor and underprivileged social groups as can be legitimately expected from enlightened rulers. With this the revolutionary perspective in rebuilding society was ruled out and the country had to settle down to a reformist, evolutionary and gradual process of modernization and development.

To achieve the real purpose of freedom the social and educational development of people even by evolutionary and reformist method, which according to theoreticians of Public Policy is called incrementalist approach[23], there was a need then for a comprehensive plan of educational development which would make optimum use of available resources. Unfortunately, no such plan/policy was available in 1947 although as a matter of fact the need for a such a plan was foreseen as early as 1937 when National Planning Committee was appointed by the Indian National Congress under Nehru. It could not, however, go ahead with the preparation of a satisfactory policy owing to the arrest of Jawaharlal Nehru in 1940. Later the stress of political events forced the Committee to wind up. Surprisingly, the attempts of the colonial British government to produce a long-term educational plan document have succeeded. The Central Advisory Board of Education under the leadership of Sir John Sargent, the then educational adviser to the Government of India, prepared a report on '*Post War Plan of Educational Development in India* (1944).' In fact, it was proposed to create a national system of education for the country over a period of 40 years (1944-84). This plan called for nothing short of liquidation of illiteracy in a period of forty years in the country. Political events then overtook everything else and the official plan never took off the ground. So the educational development of India after independence had to be planned and implemented ab initio.

Obviously this absence of comprehensive and sufficiently detailed plan to act upon was not difficult to understand. The government of free India could have appointed an Education Commission as it ultimately did in 1964. But this decision was not taken then and developments in education in the country were attempted for nearly two decades (1947-65) without any direction and firm policy. This ad-hocism is certainly one of the important factors responsible for the large spurt in illiteracy today.

The government of independent India also did not take steps to create a sufficiently critical mass of active and competent workers who could help to plan the transformation of educational system.

An examination of the inter-se priorities between different sectors of education reveals that personal and social factors played a more important role than rational choices. Nehru had great faith in universities and in higher education and believed that higher education must be developed on priority basis, in the larger interests of the country. Relatively speaking he did not show deep commitment either to elementary or adult education. Universal elementary and Adult Education ought to have been accorded the highest priority because along with adult franchise it would have helped in the process of effective political decision-making like electoral choices and through that achieve the real transfer of power to the masses which was the overt aim of the national leadership.

However, of the two sectors of education i.e. primary and adult education, the neglect of adult education was more conspicuous because primary education managed to claim a little more of attention. This was because primary education constitutes the first and indispensable rung of the ladder for formal and formally institutionalized education. In other words, primary school education forms part of the elite education system and bourgeoisie democratic cultures could not really afford to neglect the conventionally important channels of elite education i.e. education at college and university levels. In this manner, primary education, paradoxically enough satisfied both the claims of democratic conscience on the one hand, elitist demands on the other. It is not without significance that primary education was raised to the prestigious pedestal of being incorporated into the chapter on Directive Principles of State Policy of the Indian Constitution. There is no mention of the promotion of adult education in that chapter.

The other important reason advanced then and is being shared still for according low priority to adult education is that, in the long run the provision of universal elementary education was the surest way to liquidate illiteracy and that if the goal of universalising elementary education for the 6-14 age group within 10 years was achieved it would be unnecessary to launch a massive programme of Adult Education.

It would also seem apparent that no strong social and political demand was raised from any quarter to reverse the policy of according the lowest priority to adult education. The people themselves were poor and unorganized and the type of education that was provided in elementary schools and in adult education centres was not recognized by them as an acquisition of value. The opposition parties including leftists could hardly make an impact and they did not make adult education an issue in their political struggles. The only group that fought for these programmes consistently is a group of Gandhians, a few academicians and social workers.

The Government accepted the proposal of the Central Advisory Board of Education to change the nomenclature of adult education to social education in 1949. The programme was implemented as part of community development programme up to 1958-59 and later the programme was managed by the Panchayati Raj Institutions up to 1969 when the Farmer's Functional Literacy Programme which came into operation... was implemented upto 1977. The progress of these programmes can be gauged from the following table.

TABLE 3

Progress of Adult (Social) Education 1950-51 to 1975-76.*

Year	No. of Centres	Enrolment
1950-51	48,556	12,56,011
1955-56	46,091	12,82,710
1960-61	62,815	14,94,794
1965-66	2,17,912	16,37,541
1975-76	17,774	4,39,034

*Source : J.P. Naik "National Adult Education Policy" (1947-78)

The table reveals that throughout this period there were on an average about fifty thousand Adult Education Centres run either with financial assistance from the Government or on a voluntary basis and that about 12-15 lakhs adults were made literate at a small cost, the total investment in the whole programme being less than one per cent of the total educational expenditure.

The large success in Adult Education Centres during 1965-66 was mainly due to the *Gram Shikshan Mohim* in Maharashtra, a voluntary movement conducted at a very little cost which initially showed great promise but which ultimately faded away with marginal success. In 1965-66 this movement in Maharashtra accounted for 1,83,013 centres with an enrolment of 8,45,646. This did not exist in 1950-51 and if an allowance was made for it, then it would be seen that the overall position of Adult Education in the country really became worse in 1975-76.

In the sixties, many aspects of public policies came under introspection, critical evaluation, revision. This was because the sixties saw two wars fought by India, one with China in 1962 and another with Pakistan in 1965. The Chinese aggression of 1962 and the weak response of India on the occasion came as a rude shock to every one and created a mood of introspection in which the very validity of all our developmental efforts was seriously questioned. Education was no exception and people began to ask as to why we had lagged behind in education although in 1949 the educational situation in the two countries was almost similar.[24]

The Chinese success in the war made Indians credit the Chinese socio-political system with a great level of achievement. Whatever be the truth in the assessment of the Chinese situation now (particularly in view of the current denigrating reappraisal of the Chinese success by the Chinese themselves). There was no doubt that many an Indian attributed to China an all round success in development including in the field of education. The commitment of the Chinese to the revolutionary cuuse, as exemplified by the degree of mobilization in the Chinese military and civilian cadres, made Indians reflect on education as an effective mobilizer of people to certain types of enduring commitments, not necessarily ideological commitments. Thus the concept of education to the masses once again surfaced in a conspicuous manner. The Sino-Indian war challenging the existing complacence over various aspects of public policy in India was only one of the reasons for a rethkining on educational policy. There was of course, the already existing realization that a comprehensive educational policy had to be formulated in the country.

The old demand for the appointment of an Education Commission which would examine comprehensively the educational scene in our country revived. The then Minster for Education at the Centre Sri M. C. Chagla responded to the general mood and appointed the Education Commission, with Dr. D.S. Kothari, the noted Physicist and Educationist as the Chairman of the Commission.

The main issue with which the Commission was charged was to suggest a national pattern of education and the general principles and policies for the development of education at all stages and in all aspects.[25]

It may be worthwhile to recall here that the Commission was the sixth commission appointed by the Government of India. The first was the Indian Education Commission (1882) which dealt mainly with school education. It reviewed the progress of education in the country since the Education Despatch of 1854 and laid down broad guidelines of policy for the development of education over the next two decades (1882-1902). The second was the Indian University's Commission (1902) which reviewed the development of higher education since the establishment of three Universities at Bombay, Madras and Calcutta in 1857 and made recommendations for the reorganization of Indian Universities. The third was the Calcutta University Commission (1917-19) which reviewed the development of secondary and higher education in Bengal and made suggestions for the reorganization of the Calcutta University and the establishment of a new University at Dacca. The fourth, and the first to be appointed in the post-independence period was the University education (1948-49) which reviewed the development of higher education in the country and made proposals for its future expansion and improvement. A similar function for secondary education was performed by the Secondary Education Commission (1952) which was the fifth in the series.[26]

It will thus be seen that the policy, whether in the pre-indedence period or later was to look at eduction in a compartmentalised fashion and that no commission had ever been appointed for primary and adult education.

A strong demand was therefore made in the fifties, and early sixties that the Government of India should appoint a commission to look at education as a whole including adult and primary education. It was in respose to this demand that the Central Government appointed the Education Commission (1964-66) at the initiative of M.C. Chagla, the then Minister of Education at the Centre and entrusted it with the task of looking at the entire spectrum of education, except the high professional areas like legal and medical education. This was therefore, the first Commission in our educational history to look comprehensively at almost all aspects of education. The commission headed by Dr. D. S. Kothari had prepared a blue print of educational development in India spread over 20 years (1966-86).

The Commission recommended that high priority should be given to adult education and it even ambitiously set a deadline to liquidate illiteracy among adults (1986). Recognising the importance of voluntary agencies for the successful implementation of qualitative policies like Adult Education in general and developmental programmes in particular, the comission specifically said that "voluntary agencies working in these fields should be given every encouragement, financially and technically. Adult education is an area ideally suited to voluntary effort and the work to be done is of such dimensions that mobilization of this will play crucial role in the success of our plan".[27] With the report of the education commission in hand, the government took further steps in the process of formulating a national policy on education. In order to raise the subject of education above party considerations and also with a veiw to obtaining consensus among political parties, the Minister of Education Dr. Trigun Sen, constituted a Committee of Members of Parliament belonging to all political parties with the expectation that the Members of the Committee would provide a working draft of the national policy on education. It was also thought that the National Policy on Education would pave the way for national education act.

The committee of Members of Parliament received with considerable enthusiasm the recommendation of the Commissions on Adult Education. In its report it said, "the liquidation of mass illiteracy is essential, not only for accelerating programme of production, especially in agriculture but by quickening the tempo of national development in general. Plan to accelerate the spread of literacy should therefore be prepared and intensively implemented on several fronts. With a view to reducing new additions to the ranks of adult illiterates, part-time literary classes should be organized for grown-up children (age group 11-17) who did not attend school or have lapsed into illiteracy. All employees in large commercial industrial and other concerns should be made functionally literate within a prescribed period of their employment and a lead in this direction should be given by the inudustrial plants in public sector. Similarly, teachers, students and educational institutions should be actively involved in literacy campaigns, especially as a part of the social or national service programme. The achievements of literacy should be sustained by the provision of attractive reading materials and library services to the new literates".[28]

The national policy on education which was issued subsequently (1968) more or less repeats recommedations of the Members of Parliament Committee on Adult Education. The government reiterated that "the liquidation of mass illiteracy is necessary not only for promoting participation in the working of democratic institutions and for accelerating programmes of production, especially in agriculture, but for quickening the tempo of national development".[29]

The policy statement further states that 'special emphasis should be given to the education of young practicing farmers and to the training of youth for self-employment".[30]

In pursuance of the policy the Government included Adult Education in the Fourth Plan. A special programme was launched to train young farmers in high yielding technology. The Farmers Functional Literacy Programme (F F L P) which was inaugurated in 1967-68 was intended to bring a new emphasis to the concept of Adult Education by the addition of functionality component to it.

It was implemented in selected blocks in all states. Since it was tagged on to the Green Revolution—one of the most successful programmes in agriculture in India, it has succeeded to some extent. But the programe had not reached many people especially the marginal and small farmers who incidentally constitute the majority of adult illiterate population in our county.

Summary

The foregoing reveals that the policy makers have made only half-hearted attempts in tackling the problem of illiteracy among adults in our country. Immediately after independence, the programme of adult education was re-designated as social education and was implemented as part of the eommunity development programme up to 1956-57 and in the period that followed and upto 1965-66 the Panchayati Raj institutions were entrusted with the responsibility of implementing the social education programme. These institutions themselves lost their importance by the end of third plan and a new programme was formulated with a view to imparting functional literacy skills among young farmers to increase agricultural productivity. The spread of these programmes was thin and compared to magnitude of illiteracy that did not make a significant impact.

The year 1977 saw a change in the government at the Centre. The Janata Party which came to power in 1977 attempted in a big way to re-align priorities in education. In the scheme of re-alignment, adult education was accorded top priority. The policy statement which was released in 1978 on National Adult Education Programme, recognizing the need for a massive programme to educate adult illiterates. it declared that "government have resolved to wage a clearly-conceived, well-planned and relentless struggle against illiteracy to enable masses to play an active role in social and cultural change".[31] Reviewing the progress of the earlier programme, the statement recorded that "in the post independence period, the achievements in the field of literacy have been far from satisfactory. In 1947, the rate of literacy was 14 per cent which rose to 34.45 percent (excluding the age group of 0-4) in 1971. Yet, owing to the population increase and half-heartedness of the past effort, the number of illiterate persons has risen from 247 million in 1951 to 307 million in 1971".32 The statement further added that "according to the Census of 1971 the total number of illiterate persons above 14 years of age is 209.5 million of which 97.1 million are in the age group of 15-35 which is likely to be about 100 million at present. A massive programme should be launched to cover this vast segment of population in 15- 5 age group as far as possible within five years of its launching".[33] Thus the Janata Government set the dead-line of five year period (from 1978-83) to cover about 100 million adult illiterate throughout the country.

The government planned to implement the programme through a multiplicity of agencies which include governmental, voluntary, private and public sector industry and institutions for formal education. Thus the National Adult Education Programme was launched on October 2, 1978 with a goal of educating 100 million illiterates in the age group of 15-35. An outlay of Rs. 200 crores was provided in the Sixth draft Five Year Plan (1978-83) for implementing this programe.

As noted earlier a unique feature of the Janata adult education policy is the precedence given to voluntary agencies in its implementation.

The present study is an attempt to examine the process of implementation of the National Adult Education Programme through voluntary agencies for the following reasons : (1) problems in implementation of this massive adult education programme afford a rich area for the understanding of the process of public administration, (2) an understanding of the implementation enables the researcher to make policy recommendations which obviously constitute an integral part of studies in public policy and finally the implementation of adult education programme is to some extent unique as a good part of it is entrusted to non-governmental organizations, especially to voluntary agencies.

The objectives of the present study are :

(1) To study and analyse the functioning of voluntary agencies involved in National Adult Education Programme with reference to staffing pattern, recruitment and training of instructors and supervisors, supply of teaching materials, problems encountered in running adult education centres and suggestions to improve the programme.

(2) To analyse the working of adult education centres—location, facilities and functioning.

(3) To determine the socio-economic background of the learners, dropouts, and potential learners.

(4) To assess the achievement of learners in terms of lite racy and numeracy skills, the level of social awareness and improvement of functional skills of the learners all of which are the goals of the National Adult Education Programme.

(5) To analyse the socio-economic background of instructors and supervisors and its correlation with the programme and also to analyse their attitudes towards the aims and methods of the programme.

(6) To examine the general performance of the voluntary agencies in the implementation of the Programme.

Before we analyse the process of the implementation of National Adult Education Programme with above objectives in mind, an attempt would be made in the next chapter to examine the correlation between education and social change and development as a backdrop to the imperatives that are behind the evolution of adult education policy.

Methodology

The National Adult Education Progromme which was started in 1978 on a large scale throughout the country is relatively a new programme. Some studies have already been reviewed on this programme. However, most of them are quick appraisals. The objectives of the present study have already been mentioned in the previous sections. Primary and Secondary techniques of data collection are employed to study the objectives.

Primary data was collected by administering interview schedules to (1) learners, (2) dropouts and (3) potential learners and also to (4) instructors.

Published reports and other documentary sources constitute the secondary sources.

Universe

The area selected for the study is Andhra Pradesh. Andhra Pradesh occupies the 23rd position in literacy among 22 states and 10 Union territories in our country according to 1981 Census. It is one of the darkest spots on the literacy map of India wherein about 71 per cent of the total population is illiterate in all age groups. The above reasons prompted the investigator to select Andhra Pradesh as the area of study besides other logistical considerations.

The first phase of National Adult Education programme in Andhra Pradesh has been attempted for study. The programme is being implemented through five types of agencies which include (a) State Governments', (b) voluntary agencies, (c) Nehru Yuvak Kendras, (d) Universities and College and (e) Integrated Child Development Schemes.

Nine voluntary agencies were granted financial assistance by the Central Ministry of Education and Social Welfare for implementation of National Adult Education Programme in Andhra Pradesh in the first phase. The names of the agencies, the areas of operations and the number of centres sanctioned are givea in the following table.

TABLE-4

Voluntary Agencies selected for Financial Sanction, the Areas, Number of Centres

Sl.No.	Name of the Agency	Area of operation		No. of Centres
1.	Andhra Mahila Sabha, Hyderabad	Huzurnagar	100	300
		Sircilla	100	
		Jangaon	100	
2.	Andhra Pradesh Rashtra Adimajati Sevak Sangh, Vijayawada	Tenali Guntur Dt.		60
3.	Bhagavathula Charitable Trust, Yellamanchili	Yellamanchili Vizag Dt.		30
4.	Bharateeya Adimajati Sevak Sangh, Hyderabad	Narasampet		100

5.	Comprehensive Rural Operations Service Society Bhongir	Narasampet Tq.	30
6.	Durga Sangh Seva Samaj Vijayawada	Gannavaram	30
7.	Hindu Kust Nivaran Sangh Hyderabad	Jammikunta	60
8.	Village Reconstruction Organization, Guntur	Guntur Prakrsam Krishna	79/100
9.	Weaker Community Action for Development and Liberation Hyderabad.	Shadnagar Tq. Mahboobnagar Dt.	30

Source : Records of Directorate of Adult Education, Government of Andhra Pradesh. 1980-81, 1981-82, 1982-83, 1983-84.

Sample

The area of the operation of the voluntary agencies which have implemented N A E P is spread over eight districts in Andhra Pradesh, which includes Guntur, Krishna, Prakasam Visakhapatnam in what is popularly known as the coastal region of the State, and Warangal, Nalgonda, Karimnagar and Mohaboobnagar what is known as Telangana region of the State. No voluntary agency has applied for financial sanction in Rayalaseema area to implement the National Adult Education Programme in the first Phase (1979-1984).

In order to select the sample, the eight districts where the voluntary agencies have implemented the National Adult Education Programme have been classified into three categories according to the literarcy percentage. The following table gives the idea of the method adopted.

TABLE-5

Literacy Level of the Districts (1971 Census 15-35 Age group)

(in per centages)

Sl. No.	Name of the District	Male	Female	Total	Classification
1.	Krishna	54.4	38.6	47.0	I Category
2.	Guntur	54.4	30.6	42.9	Acove 40% Advanced
3.	Prakasam	46.6	18.2	32.2	II
4.	Visakhapatnam	42.4	18.4	30.3	30 per cent and above Less Advanced
5.	Warangal	39.0	13.3	26.1	III
6.	Nalgonda	37.0	12.8	25.0	Backwarkd
7.	Karimnagar	35.5	9.1	22.2	Above 20
8.	Mahboobnagar	34.2	10.5	21.9	Below 30

The eight districts were classified into three categories.

Category I : Advanced
Districts with 40 literacy percentage and above.

Category II : Less advanced
Districts with literacy percentage between 25-30 and above.

Category III : Backward
Districts with literacy percentage between 20-30.

The literacy percentage in the first category (Krishna and Guntur) is not only the highest in the sample but is also above the national average which was 29.5 per cent according to 1971 census. Sri Durga Sangh Seva Samaj was selected in the first category which has implemented National Adult Education Programme in Gannavaram block of Krishna district for the study. From the second category one agency i.e. Bhagavathula Charitable Trust (B C T) which has implemented the programme in Yellamanchili block of the Visakhapatnam district was selected. From the third category one more agency was selected, i.e. Comprehensive Rural Operations Service Society (CROSS), which has implemented the programme in Bhongir block of Nalgonda district.

In order to have a bigger sample and also to protect the representativeness of the sample it has been decided to select one more agency from the third category as it is the third category which is backward and any impact of the programme is worth studying. The agency that has been selected is Andhra Mahila Sabha, Hyderabad. Thus the total sample selected for the study consists of four voluntary organizations.

The following table gives the details of the sample.

TABLE 6.

Agencies in the Sample and the number of Adult Education Centres sanctioned

Sl. No.	Name of the Agency	Head Quarters	Area of Operation	No. of Centres sanctioned
1.	Durga Sangh Seva Samaj (DSSS)	Vijayawada Krishna Dt.	Gannavaram Block, Krishna Dt.	30
2.	Bhagavathula Charitable Trust (BCT)	Yellamanchili Vizag Dt.	Yellamanchili Block, Vizag Dt.	3C
3.	Comprehensive Rural Operation Service Society (CROSS)	Bhongir Nalgonda Dt.	Nalgonda Dt.	30
4.	Andhra Mahila Sabha (AMS)	Hyderabad	Karimnagar	100
	Total number of Centres			190

It may also be mentioned here that the sample consists of two types of organizations : Bhagavathula Charitable Trust (BCT) and Comprehensive Rural Operations Service Society (CROSS) which are general organisations and the two women's organizations, viz. Andhra Mahila Sabha (AMS) and Durga Sangh Seva Samaj (D S S). All the agencies selected have some previous experience in adult education programmes though the length of experience varies considerably.

Size of the sample

Ten per cent of the total number of centres run by the four agencies constitutes the sample of Adult Education centres for the study. The total number of adult education centres run by these four agencies in the sample are 190 and ten per cent of it comes to 19. The method followed in selecting the adult education centres in various areas is stratified purposive random sampling. The list of adult education centres under different agencies in the sample is appended.

Further the sample consists of learners, dropouts, potential learners, instructors and supervisors. The details are given below.

Learners : The prescribed strength of an adult education centre is thirty. Thus the total number of learners enrolled in 19 adult education centres comes to 570. It has been decided to take 30 per cent of the total number of enrolled which come to about 172 learners which is considered a fairly good sample.

Dropouts : Three dropouts per an adult education centre are selected through the method of incidental sampling. Their total number comes to 57 at the rate of three per centre of the 19 adult education centres.

Potential learners : At the rate of two potential learners per an Adult Education Centre in the sample the total number of potential learners in the sample comes to 38..

Instructors : All the instructors of the nineteen adult education centres' constitute the sample.

Supervisors : All the Supervisors of the four agencies constitute the sample for the study.

Project Officers : All the Project Officers of the four agencies come under the sample. The following table gives the details of the sample.

TABLE 7

Category of Respondents

	AMS	RCT	CROSS	DSS	Total
Learners	90	27	27	27	171
Dropouts	30	9	9	9	57
Potential Learners	20	6	6	6	38
Instructors	10	3	3	3	19
Supervisors	1	1	1	1	4
Project Officers	1	1	1	1	4
Director of Adult Education	—	—	—	—	1
Asst. Director (Voluntary Agencies)	—	—	—	—	1
Project Officers	—	—	—	—	2
Total responder.ts					297

List of Adult Education Centres/Villages in the Sample is appended.

The limitations of the study and profiles of the voluntary agencies in the same follow.

Study of Agencies Limitations

Empirical studies suffer from certain limitations. Apart from their tendency to jump to conclusions they exhibit a proneness to generalization. This study also has had to reckon with this limitation, though it has tried to minimise it. Some of the limitations of this study are mentioned hereunder :

First, the agencies were selected on the basis of 1971 Census literacy statistics in the districts as the 1981 Census had not beed published at the time of the commencement of the study. On comparison with 1981 Census it was found that the literacy profile is broadly continuing.

Second, the focus was mainly on voluntary agencies. In the districts where the agencies carried out their programme, there were other agencies like the State Government, Universities and Colleges, Nehru Yuvak Kendras and welfare departments engaged in similar programmes. But owing to logistical constraints, no comparative analysis has been attempted, although the investigator is aware of its advantages specially in respect of such questions as that of the dropouts.

Third, though structured interview schedules were prepared for the Principal Officers of the Voluntary Agencies, they failed to elicit the kind of response which was expected due to several factors like the non-availability of most of the office-bearers and the tendency of those available to be evasive in their replies. That is why after the pre-testing stage itself it was given up and in its place an interview guide was prepared to gather the views of office bearers on N A E P.

Fourth, only the essential aspects of the programme were studied without losing sight of the programme as a whole because of lack of time. The study does not claim to be exhaustive either in its administrative or policy aspects, since it has concerned itself mainly with such important aspects as co-ordination which are considered central to its objective.

Coming to the analysis part of the study the investigator has not employed any highly sophisticated statistical tests to quantify the data but only fairly simple statistical techniques.

Finally, in determining the impact of the programme the schedule on learners was administered only once to the respondents. In other words, it is not a longitudinal study, i.e. the investigator has not visited the centres more than once. It may be true that the process of learning or the ability to learn can be gauged more accurately if longitudinal method of enquiry is adopted, i.e. spread over a period of a year or the length of a programme like the month stipulated of N A E P.

As for field problems, the investigator has faced such problems as are usually encountered in such studies.

In spite of adequate planning like informing the office-bearers of the sample agencies well in advance the investigator faced the problems of the non-availability of the officers, which did upset the time schedule of the investigator.

Again, the researcher encountered the problem of determining the age of the respondents, especially the learners, potential learners and dropouts. The age as revealed by the respondents or as reported is not supported by evidence. The investigator tried to cross-check the data by asking the village headman in several cases. The investigator had doubts about the veracity of age as given out by the respondents on a good number of cases, since it belied their appearance.

Again in spite of his best efforts, the researcher failed to establish rapport with some of the respondents who viewed his mission with suspicion. Some thought that the investigator was a Government official and treated him as they would a Tahsildar or a Police Officer. In both instances the researcher found it difficult to communicate with the respondents effectively.

Rural women were heistant, frightened and shy of talking to the researcher.

Owing to migration of some villagers, the researcher was forced to re-draw his sample repeatedly. In some cases the researcher could not persuade them to respond to the schedule and in others found them hostile.

Profiles of the Agencies in the Sample

1. **Andhra Mahila Sabha (A M S)**

The Andhra Mahila Sabha was established in 1937. The activities of the Andhra Mahila Sabha are varied and cover a wide range of social services including extension of medical services, training of nurses, training of women in handicrafts, education for girls from the pre-primary level to the college level, teachers' education, adult literacy and condensed courses of education of girls and adult women. The Literacy House established in 1972 is the principal wing of the A M S primarily engaged in Adult Education and literacy programmes.

The main objectives of the A M S are (1) to train earnest and efficient workers and harness their services for the progress of Indian women, (2) to promote education of women, (3) to promote the health and education of children, (4) to establish and maintain hospitals and nursing homes for women and (5) to undertake programmes of adult education and literacy in general.

The first Literacy House was established in Lucknow, the second was set-up in Hyderabad mainly because of the untiring efforts of the late Dr. (Mrs) Durga Bai Deshmukh, the well-known freedom fighter, Gandhian and social worker of India.

The Sabha first took up the Farmers Functional Literacy Project in one of the backward districts in Andhra Pradesh in the third quarter of the sixties. The Government of Andhra Pradesh subsequently involved the Mahila Sabha in a big way in running ten projects in various districts. Thus the Andhra Mahila Sabha (A M S) has acquired considerable experience in the sphere of Adult Education.

2. **Bhagavathula Charitable Trust (B C T)**

Though formally registered in 1976 the B C T has been well-known in Yellamanchili area since the mid sixties. It came to prominence in recent years thanks to the efforts of Dr. B.V. Parameswara Rao, a scientist-engineer turned voluntary social worker.

Starting with the establishment of a High School in 1967, it soon expanded its activities with the setting up of a salt factory in 1969 with the help of Andhra Pradesh Small Scale Industries Development Corporation, a Co-operative Farmers' Service Centre in 1974 and a Cattle Cross Breeding Farm in 1975. In addition, it sponsored several income and employment generating projects, some of which, as stated in one of of its annual reports, were scuttled by powerful local vested interests.

Thus the B C T runs a host of economic programmes. Broadly guided by Sarvodaya philosophy, this agency endeavours to associate the villagers with most of its programmes and projects. For instance, the agency mobilised about five hundred villagers for the diversion of Godavari Waters in 1982. Undaunted by the machinations of local politicians the agency could forge ahead with its plans and policies.

The main objectives of the agency as can be gleaned from its annual report include (i) to develop small, marginal farmers, landless labourers, artisans, women and youth ; (ii) to serve as a 'catalyst' and an educator for the development of its clientele ; (iii) to explore the possibilities for the use of local resources and relevant technologies ; (iv) to train man power ; (v) to build up local leadership with a view to enabling them to handle their problems ; (vi) to encourage self-help and group action ; (vii) to continuously endeavour for bringing in innovations and new strategies for rural development.

The operational sphere of the agency extends to about 60 villages in and around Yellamanchili (50 kilometers from the port city of Visakhapatnam).

Since 1976, the agency has made considerable progress in rural development and is heading for a big breakthrough with its expansion programme.

Thus B.C.T. simultaneously is engaged in several economic and educational programmes.

3. Comprehensive Rural Operations Service Society (C R O S S)

With its headquarters at Bhongir (35 kilometers from Hyderabad) the Comprehensive Rural Operations Service Society was established in 1975. Its main aim is to carry out comprehensive development programmes in rural areas for the development of the poor by the poor irrespective of caste and religion. The major target group is that of Harijans who are economically most backward. Some of the important activities include (i) adult education, (ii) community organization, (iii) development of the irrigation water sources, (iv) dairy development and other economic programmes, (vi) rural medical education and services and (vi) agriculture extension services.

Its areas of operation are spread over 150 villages around Bhongir, Motkur and other taluqs in Nalgonda district and functions through village 'Sanghams'. Education, particularly adult education, constitutes an important part of the developmental package.

4. Durga Sangh Seva Samaj (D S S)

Located in Vijayawada (about 350 kilometers from Hyderabad) and established in the sixties, Durga Sangh Seva Samaj is one of the earliest women's organisations in Andhra Pradesh. Its main objective is to encourage women to acquire formal educational qualifications like of matriculation and graduation. The agency also trains women in tailoring, embroidery and other crafts. Funded programmewise by the State Government Women's financial and welfare agencies and the Central Social

Welfare Boards, this agency is managed by a few women workers. The overall administration is looked after by a retired Headmaster.

Except helping needy women with scholarships, coaching them for various examinations, the agency does not seem to undertake any major programmes. However, the agency is committed to the upliftment ef women.

NOTES AND REFERENCES

1. Carl Friedrich, *Man and His Government* (New York : McGraw Hill 1963) p. 18.
2. Richard Rose, "*Policy Making in Great Britain* (London : Macmillan, 1969), os quoted in Andreson, "Public Policy Making" (New York : Praeger, 1975) p. 2.
3. Robert Eyestone, *The Threads of Public Policy : A Study in Policy Leadership*, (Indianpolis : Bobbs—Merril 1971) p. 21.
4. Thomas R. Dye, *Understanding Pablic Policy* (Prentice—Hall Inc, 1978) p. 63.
5. James Anderson, *Public Policy Making* (New York : Praeger, 1972) p. 12.
6. See David Easton, *Political System : A framework for Polttical Analysis* (Englewood Cliffs : N.J. Prentice Hall, 1965).
7. See James E Anderson, For an interesting discussion on the role of bureaucracy, in Public Policy Making.
8. See Frank J Godnow, *Politics aud Administration* (New York : Russel & Russel, 1900). Quoted in James Anderson, *op. cit*. p. 99.
9. See Hayek, *Road to Serfdom* (London : Routledge & Kegan Paul, 1979).
10. See Von Mises, *Road to Freedom*.
11. Milton Esman, *Politics of Development Administration* in John Montgomery & William Siffins (ed) "Approaches to Development" (New York ; McGraw Hill, 1966) p. 144.
12. *Ibid*, p. 149.
13. *Ibid*, p. 156.
14. S.R. Mohisini, *Adult & Community Education : An Indian Experiment* (New Delhi : Indian Adult Education Association, 1972) p. 21.
15. M.K. Gandhi, *My Views on Education* in Hingroni (ed), (Gandhi) Peace Foundation, 1970) p. V.
16. *Ibid*, p. VII.
17. *Ibid*.
18. Nikil Ranjan Roy, *Adult Education in India and Abroad* (New Delhi ; S. Chand and Company, 1967) p. 23.

19. M.K. Gandhi, *Constructive Programme* (Ahmedabad : Navjeevan Publications, 1957) p. 27.
20. J.P. Naik, *National Education Policy, 1947-78*, (New Delhi : Government of India, Ministry of Education and Culture, 1979) p. 27.
21. *Ibid*, p. 21.
22. *Ibid*, p. 43.
23. See Charles E Lindblom, *Policy Making Process* (New Jersey ; Prentice Hill Inc. 1968) p. 41.
24. J.P. Naik, *op. cit.* p. 80.
25. *Resolution of Government of India, No F. (43), 64 E. 1.* Ministry of Education dt. 14.1.1964, New Delhi, p. 2.
26. J.P. Naik, *The Education Commission and After* (New Delhi ; Allied Publishers, 1982) p. 75.
27. Report of Education Commission. *Education and National Development* (Chairman, D.S. Kothari) New Delhi : Manager, Government of India Publications, 1978, pp. 388-403.
28. *Report of the Committee of Members of Parliament on Education Commission*, Ministry of Education, quoted in J.P. Naik, "Education Commission, and After", *op. cit.* p. 67.
29. Government of India, Ministry of Educatipn, *National Policy on Education, 1968* : Manager, Government of India Publications, New Delhi. 1969, p. 2.
30. *Ibid.*
31. National Adult Education Programme : *An Outline*, Ministry of Education and Culture, New Delhi, 1978, p. 3.
32. *Ibid*, p. 6.
33. *Ibid*, p. 7.

2

Role of Education in Social Change and Economic Development

PART–I

'Education is the key that unlocks the door to modernization.'[1] Once regarded as an essentially conservative, culture preserving, culture transmitting institution, the educational system of today has come to be viewed as a major determinant of social, political and economic change.

There are many reasons for according top priority to education in the world, and in particular, in developing countries. But some of the major developments in the last five decades which account for this new value attached to education and for shift in perspective regarding its relationship to society, the economy and the policy are : firstly the large scale entry into the world arena after decolonization of the third world countries and the consequent increase in the demand for education in those countries and secondly the increasing awareness even in the advanced countries, about the necessity to continuously educate people to cope with the technological advancement.

Education is also perceived to be one of the instruments of social change in all the developing countries. The whole gamut of literature on social change, places a high premium on the role of education as the most important vehicle for social change. However, the emphasis on education in contemporary times does not mean that education was not given its due place in earlier times. Scholarly concern with the relationship between education and other fields of social interaction is not new. Since Plato and Aristotle, political philosophers have affirmed principles embodied in the phrases, "as is the State so is the School", or "what you, want in the State, you must put into the School".[2] In other words, political thinkers too recognized the nexus between the educational and political system.

Since the 18th century, and the age of enlightenment, in particular, the role of education as liberator of mankind has come to be recognized. As 20th century and the age of democracy advanced, the faith in education as the liberator of mankind increased. The views of the conservatives and liberals are apt to be mentioned here.

While conservatives essentially believed that the purpose of education was to preserve and transmit certain values, the liberals believed that the school as an institution can play an important role in social reform for improving the lot of mankind. According to John Dewey, the noted educational philosopher : "It is the business of school environment to eliminate so far as possible, the unworthy features of the existing environment from influence upon mental habitudes...As society became more enlightened it realized that it was responsible not to transmit and conserve the whole of its existing achievements but to strive for a better future society. The school is its chief agency for the accomplishment of this end"[3].

In more recent times the famous Kothari Commission on Education arrived at the conclusion that "what is needed is a revolution in education which will set in motion the much desired social, economic and cultural revolution".[5]

However, the limits to this optimism need to be pointed out. The Marxists' notion is that while education is an effective instrument to bring the desired change, the educational system itself will only be serving vested interests i.e. status quo is a well known idea that qualifies the optimistic role attributed by Dewey. Then there is another notion, partly the off-shoot of Marxist notion, that formal education organized and promoted by the conventional social system is counter productive. The well known de-schoolers such as Reimer, Ivan Illich, Holt and Goodman attacked the present forms of education and called for alternative strategies in education which can lead to transformation of society towards desirable objectives of freedom to enjoy life, liberty and pursuit of happiness for all. Ivan Illich in particular argued that schooling is one of the major means by which status quo is preserved.[6]

Endorsing the view of Illich, Kurien, an Indian scholar, brought out nicely how knowledge (and hence education that is geared to imparting knowledge) "becomes the cleverest and the most powerful ally to the status quo in all societies every where".[7]

Bertrand Russell, even earlier, had gone further and argued that "education in the modern world tends to be a reactionary force, supporting the government when it is conservative and opposing it when it is progressive".[8]

In the words of Harold Silver, a contemporary scholar, "education has been seen both as a means of selecting and perpetuating elites. It is discussed in terms of class domination and social control but also of social liberation and progress... It has become more and more prominent in political manifestos and policies in economic calculation and family discussions, in book shops and in the press. It has also become a major instrument of national policy. Educational systems and educationists have come together in educational movements, professional conferences and in attempts at educational policy at regional, national and international levels. Education has become one of the most sensitive national responses to economic and political change.[9]

Education and Economic Development

If education is regarded as a prerequisite for social change, facilitating reorientation of values through better understanding of the environment, human, material and physical, it is regarded as directly promotive of economic advancement also.

The human investment revolution in economic thought initiated in 1960's by Theodore Schultz[10] produced an electrifying effect on the trends theory and practice of education. Education has come to be regarded a panacea for all the ills in society.

The governments of the world, particularly third world, were convinced of the economic benefits of education. The approach to education was changed ; from consumption or a device for culture transmission to as 'the most valuable investment in mankind' which pays the best dividend. Concepts like investment in man and 'human capital' swept into developmental plans of countries. "Education plans were drawn as part of social and economic development plans".[11] Slogans like 'universal elementary education', 'man power planning', 'investment in man' were heard all over.

Some of the works reviewed here show how education and economic development are inter-linked.

Education is regarded as a prerequisite for economic growth.[12] The acceptance of education as the master determinant of long-term economic growth, apart from all its other benefits in the development process, has become for many persons almost an article of faith. T.W. Schultz in a paper opined that "except for some pure rent (in earning) for differences in the inherited abilities most of the differences in earnings are a consequence of differences in the amounts that have been invested in people".[13]

Although investment in people consists of such other factors as improvement in health, increasing the output of foodgrains etc., the major component of investment in human being is in the form of more and better education.

Education is regarded as a consumption good and a production good at the same time. Even those who are never engaged in any of the occupation for the performance of which they may have received education probably have gained enormously by their educational experience in that they have access to more and different forms of consumption which they would not have had without this education. Of course, the developed countries which do not have to worry about the subsistence sector may view the role of education in this perspective. But in developing countries although some returns from investment in education may be expected at all stages of economic development, investment in educational facilities may produce much lower returns in some earlier stages of economic growth that the application of equal amounts of investment in other forms of capital especially capital constituting the material infrastructure of an economy. For example, the development of more roads or the construction of more dams for increasing power generation or increasing the irrigated area at early stages of development yield substantially higher returns than equal amounts of investment in education. It is an extreme case of deferred investment.

In terms of net returns on various forms of investment outlay, we may distinguish different phases in a developing country. At certain periods, investments in a given set of non-human resources and at other periods investment in human resources bring about a higher sustained rate of growth of average income. However. we must distinguish between not only outlays on investment in human capital against non-human capital but also outlays on different sectors of human resource development (for example, investment in higher education which is investment in high level non-power and non-formal education).

Broadly speaking economic development is the result of two factors : the human factor and the non-human factor (using the word non-human in a purely technical sense).[14] It is the human factor which contributes to more then 50 per cent of economic growth which has taken place in different countries.

Literacy and Economic Development

The UNESCO publication of 1964 described the economic and social aspects of educational planning as a subject 'which is topical, important and a relatively new field of study'.[15] Many may argue that literacy is not to be the same thing as education, involving various levels and kinds. Carlo M. Cippola in his work 'Literacy and Development' after analysing the interaction between literacy and the industrial revolution, came to the conclusion that "Had literacy remained the well-guarded monopoly of a few mandarins, European society would hardly have developed in the way it did. The industrial revolution was not the product of one or two high priests of science, it was the outcome of the daily down-to-earth experiments and tinkering on the part of a number of literate craftsman and amateur scientists."[16] Economic development depends upon several factors like natural resources, technological progress, social structure, education etc. Keeping in mind this broad framework, one can say that the growth of literacy and industrialization are to a degree, correlated. There are two perspectives that determine these. Some say industrialization generates additional resources and needs more manpower, thereby facilitating growth in literacy. Others would say that industrialization presupposes a fairly widespread literacy. Countries with a high rate of literacy are those which imported the industrial revolution. Widespread literacy meant not only an elastic supply of literate workers but also a more receptive approach to life on the part of the population.[17]

The western experience, by and large, shows that a large reserve of literacy constitutes an essential base for industrialization. Industrialization might quicken the pace of literacy but a fairly high degree of literacy would be necessary for industrialization. One can hardly stress the point that depending upon their natural resources, technological progress and historical context, different countries show different time lags and rates of development. The correlation between literacy and per capita income cannot, therefore, be uniform between countries or between different periods in respect of a given country.

More studies have been made to assert that "schooling and level of economic development are highly correlated around the world." For example, Harbison and Myers (1964) report that about 75 nations G N P per capita correlated. .67 with primary school enrolment, .82 with secondary school enrolment and .74 with third level enrolment. McClelland (1966) has shown elsewhere that countries which invested heavily in secondary education, developed more rapidly on an average economically a number of years later when the educated population would have reached its peak capacity in the work force. It looks as though more of every kind of education would pay in the long run apart from generating that economic growth.[18]

Correlation between literacy and economic development is thus no longer a matter of vision or hunch but something supported by wide-ranging historical and contemporary social science research.

Delineating the gains of literacy, a Soviet Social Scientist stated that "consideration of the salaries and productivity of different categories of manual and other workers in relation to their educational qualifications, showed conclusively that even the most elementary school education is much more beneficial to a worker than a similar period of practical training at the bench. In making these observations one has to keep in mind several factors such as the age, the professional experience and the technical qualifications. Citing an example, the Soviet specialist wrote that elementary instruction gained in one year of primary education increases a worker's productivity by 30 per cent, on an average whereas, the improvement in qualification of illiterate workers and the increase in their output, resulting from a similar period of apprenticeship at a factory, is only 12 to 16 per cent a year. The improvement in qualification resulting from one year's education at school, is on the average, 2.6 time greater than that resulting from one year's apprenticeship. After four years of primary education worker's output and wages are 72 per cent higher than those of the first category worker who has had no schooling.[19] If we combine literacy acquired through formal schooling (broadly first level education) and literacy acquired through adult education involving, say, a rudimentary instruction of one year, the additional output, it was stated in the article, would be 17 per cent in the former category and 30 per cent in the latter.

A more recent and enlightening piece of research by William A. Harzog Jr. on 'Literacy and Community Economic Development in Rural Brazil' holds good for India also. He cited 21 variables such as age, schooling, home improvement, income, milk production, farm size, economic knowledge, radio listening, information sources, mass media credibility, change agent contact, social participation, opinion leadership, occupational aspirations, future attitude, achievement motivation, empathy, credit-attitude, risk orientation, innovativeness and participation, and concludes that "for the Brazilian farming sample, community economic level is positively related to community literacy level."[20] The author used a large sample of Brazilian farmers divided into four groupings according to the level of community development.

These findings taken together lend firm support to the suggestion that literacy has played a significant role in the unfinished green revolution in India. States like Punjab, Haryana, parts of U.P., Gujarat, Maharashtra, and the coastal Andhra, Karnataka, Tamil Nadu and Kerala which have registered good results in this regard, barring Haryana and some parts of Andhra Pradesh, happen to have a percentage of literacy higher than the All-India average. Assam, West Bengal, Bihar, Orissa, Rajasthan, Madhya Pradesh which are still practically beyond the reach of the green revolution barring West Bengal to have a percentage of literacy lower than the all-India average. Of course, some say that, literacy is just one variable, however significant, and that other factors (cultural patterns, irrigation facilities, political conditions etc.) have to be taken into account for arriving at a correct assessment. The observations made by Ziolkowski in his study also deserve mention here. "Great achievements in agricultural development have been brought about in regions where the level of literacy and education...are high."[21]

In another piece of research 'Education of young farmers and its impact on Agricultural production,' the author, J.S. Parolkar has attempted a quantitative correlation between education and production. He found that "Quantitative estimates of the role played by education in increasing production reveals that there is a significant correlative between crop yield and education. Total variation in crop yield accounted for the variables viz. adoption of improved farm practices, participation in extension education activities, per capita land holding and general literacy education is 67 per cent out of which literacy education alone is responsible for 21 per cent. He added that while in the use of more literacy there may be some deferred but indefinite values, functional literacy would yield quicker and more concrete results. 'It is beyond doubt, he wrote, that a certain level and quality of literacy education background of a farmer has significant relationship with their agricultural production.'[22]

It is not out of place here to mention an Indian study by A. R.Desai and S.P. Paralkar titled 'The Relationship between Literacy and Economic Productivity of Industrial Workers of Bombay : A sociological analysis'. The findings of the study indicate that in general, literates seemed more responsible to means of working to improve their conditions ; literate workers consider themselves much more self-reliant in the important domestic and civic activities like shopping, helping children in their studies, reading newspapers, voting in elections etc. Illiterate workers are liable to infringe rules more frequently by their ignorance and have no defence against exploitation etc. Literates showed greater initiative and adaptability in learning new skills, have good acquaintance with co-operative credit societies and medical benefits and in the opinion of 45 out of 50 supervisors interviewed by one investigator, it was found that literacy instutitions would improve the workers's performance by making them aware of the technical and organizational principles at work in the factory and how one's own effort contributes to the total production process.[23]

A more detailed study on 'Economics of Education' conducted by M. Blaug concludes that "the effect of literacy is to provide people with an additional means of communication. In this way also literacy may contribute to economic development by (1) raising the productivity of new literates, (2) raising the productivity of individuals working in association with literates, (3) facilitating and expediting the flow of general knowledge of individuals (e.g. information about health, nutrition etc.) and demand for thus reducing the cost of useful information, (4) stimulating the vocational training and technical education, (5) acting as a device for selecting the more able and enhancing their occupational mobility and (6) strengthening economic incentives meaning the tendency of people to respond positively to a rise in the rate of reward for their benefits.[24]

However, more recently, there has been a departure from the optimism implicit in the correlation between economic development and literacy and education and economic development. The results of empirical research conducted in the developed countries have led to the view that education may in fact have little effect either on productivity or on income distribution.[25] Instead, education has been regarded by some merely as a screening device, a convenient but expensive means of labelling people which makes no direct contribution to increased productivity as such.[26]

A less extreme view is that, the schooling confers economic benefits not by improving cognitive ability as such but by inculcating certain habits such as punctuality and discipline that are valued by employers and by society at large.[27] Yet, others those who belong to the Marxist school, maintain that effects of education on inequality themselves depend on the mode of production within which the educational system operates... in a class society education may be a device for perpetuating economic inequality between classes and income groups.[28]

The other writers who doubt the positive relationship between education and literacy are Bauman and Anderson who suggested that "although there are positive correlations between education and economic levels, these connection are loose ones."[29]

The thrust of their argument with regard to literacy was that while literacy upto 30 to 40 per cent 'is a prerequisite" to higher per capita income, there was no such correlation over the 30 to 70 per cent range.

Nevertheless, as far as the role of education, specifically in the developing countries is concerned, the benefits of schooling and spread of literacy still generally prevail though this point needs further elaboration.

Chanchal Sarkar, the well known analyst and journalist, in an article drew interesting conclusions on various aspects of population policy. According to him "A population policy for most people including the policy makers, usually signifies a clinical effort to prevent birth. And here, perhaps as much as any where, we are missing the boat. A population should mean so much more than a clinical effort. It should be a policy about education, employment, ecology, about the status of women and their opportunities, about instilling confidenc in society that progress is possible and desirable. Population policy also touches and is affected by tax law, the law of inheritance, subsidies and allowance, social service allocations, the urban rural balance of development and hundred other areas of economic, fiscal and social policy".[30] He wrote that "literacy (and education) has relevance for most of these things employment, ecology, status of women, will to improve, urban rural balance etc".

In a perceptive study about the relationship between demographic variables, health services and education in Kerala, Gopinathan Nair observed that the decline in birth rate in Kerala began before the intensification of the family planning programme.[31] He concluded that 'if as our study indicates education together with widespread public health facilities is an essential pre-condition for bringing down the birth rate, it might be appropriate to direct more resources to extension education and public health facilities along with popularization of family planning'.[32]

Education as an essential input for social transformation has also been touched upon by several writers. Notable among those who reflected on this aspect is Paulo Freire.[33] In two outstanding scholarly works 'Pedagogy of the Oppressed' and 'Cultural Action for Freedom', Frerie showed how education constitute in a critical input bringing about the desired change or transformation in people which is so necessary for initiating the process of change. Calling for revolution in the process of learning, he suggested that the one way method of teaching must be given up in favour of dialogue oriented education. Characterizing the muteness and putting up with misery by millions of people as 'culture of silence' he called for conscientization of people to make them aware of realities surrounding them and fight relentlessly against exploitation. Education in this connection 'conscientizatlon' he says alone would liberate the poor from exploitation. Richard Shaull in his foreword to the book "Pedagogy of the Oppressed" is right when he worte that Paulo Freire's work represents a new unity of theory and praxis.[34] It must be said that the contributions of Paulo Freire continue to attract the attention of academics in methods of learning as well as teaching.

Thus the review of some of the studies reveals that education plays a significant role in economic, social, political and cultural develoment of a country. How much importance should education be given in a country is debatable to some extent. But by and large the social scientists, analysts and others concerned admit that education does play an important role in the development of a country.

PART II

Survey of Literature : Review of Studies on National Adult Education Programme

As an emerging field of social science research, adult education has not yet established any considerable body of research literature.[35] Much of the research is concerned with localized surveys. Although certain aspects of adult education have been studied in depth, it has not always been to the extent that permits valid generalizations, nor has adult education been adequately conceptualized so as to indicate fruitful lines of investigation. Most of the existing research is descriptive and consists largely of surveys. Local historical studies are almost as numerous as local status surveys. These studies treat the history of adult education within an area. For example, Mohsini's work on adult and community education broadly describes the origin, growth and functioning of Jamia Millia and its place in the adult education movement in India.[36]

Case studies are another from of research in studies on adult education. A prime instance of this is the Gram Sikshan Mohim's experiment in Maharashtra the success of which received very wide publicity.

The survey of literature on adult education will be presented in two or three main categories of studies.

(1) General macro level studies on the evolution of adult education policy in India.

(2) Studies of a more particularistic nature relating to the implementation of Adult Education Programme that were in vogue before N A E P came into existence in 1978.

(3) Micro level studies on the implementation of programmes under N A E P.

Of these three, this study is more immediately concerned

with studies coming under category three. However, it is felt advisable to refer to other investigations about pre-N A E P programme implementation also.

The main types of studies concerning adult education include participation, organisation, learning process of adults, programme planning, instructional processes and evaluation. These are also major areas of research. Many studies were undertaken in each of these areas.

There are studies dealing with evolution of educational policies in India. However, as it is not possible to survey all the literature, the present survey includes a few selected studies.

J.P. Naik in his monumental work on National Educational Policy (1947-1979) studied the evolution of educational policy, of the pre and the post-independent India.[37] Analysing the cause for low achievement in the educational field, Naik carried out a comprehensive study which gives a perspective for the development of educational policy in India.

The Report of the Education Commission 1964-66 published under the title "Education and National Development" was a turning point in India's educational history. Over a decade and a half since its publication, the educational profile of this country has undergone significant changes. J.P. Naik in the book "The Education Commission and After"[38] thoroughly analysed the implementation of the recommendations of the Education Commission. Along with the recommendations on other sectors of education, the author has examined the position of the Commission on Adult Education, the translation of the recommendations on Adult Education into National Policy on Education of 1968. Quoting figures pertaining to Adult Education, gathered from various sources, the author concluded that a lesser priority was accorded to Adult Education in spite of Kothari Commission's recommendations to the contrary.

Now an attempt would be made to present a brief survey of literature which is more particularistic in nature relating to the implementation of adult education programmes that were in vogue before National Adult Education Programme came into existence in 1978. Here again the survey is limited to some studies only.

In an evaluative study of the adult education programme in Maharashtra[39] the author attempted to measure the impact of literacy component which is the main aspect of the programme on learners. The other objective was to investigate the quantitative spread and qualitative impact of the programme on the life of the people.

Some of the variables which the study included were literacy, social attitudes, participation in co-operatives, change in living patterns, awareness of responsibilities, improvement in economic status, physical standards of life, indicators of increase in knowledge and general I Q level. The study conducted in Wardha district consists of a sample of 250 female learners. The study was conducted in seven blocks. The main findings include : (1) The adult education programme did not bring the expected change in the target group in spite of the best efforts of the government. The author traced the cause of this to the apathy and indifference of the people towards literacy programmes and also the failure on the part of the organisers of the programme to motivate the adults. (2) The villagers preferred to spend their leisure time in religious and other activities rather than in social activites. (3) The Adult Education Programme had not brought any change in the life styles of the people.

These findings, though discouraging, point out the fact that a mere literacy drive without any relevance to the day-to-day life of adult illiterates is incapable of bringing the desired change in the attitude and life-style of villagers.

There are some gaps in this work. Firstly, the author did not probe much into the organizational aspects of the programme like the general attitudes of the administrators of the programme, the administrative frame-work of the programme, instructors' motivation, learner's preferences etc.

Johnson[40] in an interesting study touched several policy issues relating to adult education programme. His study is based on secondary data. He stressed the need for a re-alignment in investment priorities in education giving neglected sectors like primary education and adult education programmes a priority. The author vivdly portrayed the status of adult literacy programme in Tamil Nadu. Reviewing the performance of social education programme[41] the researcher cautioned the policy makers about the inadvisability of offering economic incentives to attract learners. The implication, perhaps, is unless 'demand' for education is felt by people themselves the adult education programmes may not succeed to the extent desired. The study demonstrated the basic weaknesses of social education programme and offers many suggestions.

The author appears to have relatively neglected investigation into various other aspects of an adult education programme like planning, co-ordination and financing. Nonetheless the study raises some important and critical questions about the place and significance of the adult education programmes.

Studies on Gram Sikshan Mohim, a programme run on voluntary basis, too constitute a part of the survey.

The Directorate of Education, Maharashtra in collaboration with Planning Commission conducted a survey of the work done under the '*Gram Shikshan Mohim*' in order to find out the achievements in regard to the eradication of illiteracy as well as the achievements in the field of all-sided development of the villages. For the purpose of the evaluation survey, 63 villages were selected by random sampling, out of 1256 villages covered under the scheme. The people in the sample villages were classified into three categories, namely, literates, semi-literates and illiterates. The survey has revealed that there were 43.1 per cent literates, 37 per cent semi-literates and 18.1 per cent total illiterates in the total sample. It was also found that the adults who became literate under the scheme had reported some change in their outlook and in the standard of living. The report recorded the positive impact of the programme on the people of those areas where it has been introduced and fully implemented. However, the report pointed out that unless post-literacy programmes are planned to the neo-literates the whole programme will go a waste.[42]

During the mid sixties the idea of linking education to the development particularly for increasing agricultural production received world-wide attention. This was in consequence to the launching of World Literacy Programme with the aim of "increasing productivity by continuing (and combining) literacy instruction with vocational training in 'technology–dependent' agricultural practices."[43]

Sponsored by U N E S C O and U N D P the well-known international agencies, this programme coincided with and in many cases, provided the educational support to what is popularly known as Green Revolution.

In the field of adult literacy this led to the emergence of the concept, and later a programme called functional literacy or work-oriented literacy. Based on this concept a project called Farmers Functional Literacy (FFL) was introduced which formed one of the components of the integrated programme of Farmers Training and Functional Literacy (FTFL). In India this was jointly sponsored by the Ministries of Food and Agriculture, Information and Broadcasting and Education, aimed at providing the needed inputs to the farmers engaged in the cultivation of high yielding varieties crops.

Initially this programme was taken up on a pilot basis in districts of India and later on it became one of the important non-formal educational programmes.

Studies on Farmers Functional Literacy Programme (FFLP) thus constitute a distinct category of studies in adult education. Some of the important studies are reviewed here.

This programme as has already been pointed out was implemented in selected blocks throughout the country. The impact of the programme on beneficiaries target groups was evaluated in Andhra Pradesh by a researcher.[44]

The main objectives of the evaluation are, to examine :

(1) the level of attainment of literacy skills,
(2) the level of agricultural knowledge acquired,
(3) the change in attitudes towards agricultural practices.

A schedule was designed to test the reading, writing and arithmatic (3R's) ability as well to elicit their opinion on changes in agricultural and general change in attitudes.

A pre-test, post-test experimental design with a time gap of one year was used for investigation. The sample consists of 540 adult participants attending Farmers Functional Literacy Centres. The sample also includes 270 illiterate adults who have not participated in the programme and treated them as participants in the control group. The researcher has chosen certain standard variables like age, caste, and farm size besides their socio-economic status to determine the impact of the programme on the participants.

The following are some of the main findings of this study.

(1) The study reported a significant difference in the achievement of literacy between the participants in the experimental group and the participants in the control group.
(2) The study found out that the participants in experimental group had acquired significant knowledge in modern agricultural methods compared to non-participants. In other words, the positive impact of the Farmers' Functional Literacy Programme (FFLP) programme has been reported.
(3) The study established the correlation between age and retention ability. So it was proved that the age of the participants was inversely related to the retention ability of the participants.
(4) The study recorded a significant, increase in the achievement and retention of literacy skills and those in modern agricultural methods with the increase in the socio-economic structure of the participants.
(5) The researcher conclusively proved that the programme had significant impact in changing the attitudes of participants towards modern agricultural methods and literacy and this could be found among all age groups, caste groups, land holding groups and in fact in all socio-economic categories.

Thus the above study reveals the effectiveness of Farmers Functional Literacy Programme.

Khan in another study examined the implementation of the Social Educational Programme in the two states.[45] The field study consists of survey in four districts of Bombay and Mysore states. The study found that the programme was not quite effective and traces the cause for this mainly in the short duration of the instructional time. From this finding he comes to the conclusion that unless the instructional time is extended from 100 hours to 200 hours the programme would not result in any appreciable benefits to the illiterate adults. The study demonstrated through empirical evidence the phenomenon of majority of neo-literates relapsing into illiteracy in a short time after the completion of the 100 hour programme.

The author further suggested that in order to sustain the interest of neo-literates vigorous efforts be made to distribute literature in simple language on relevant topics to them.

The Functional Literacy Project in Lucknow district was evaluated by the Central Ministry of Education and the Central Directorate of Adult Education. The pilot evaluation study conducted was in the district of Lucknow which is one of the three districts where the programme was introduced for the first time. The study attempted to determine the extent to which the objectives of Functional Literacy were achieved. It was observed in the study that higher the literacy level, the more is the retention of knowledge imparted and a little more increase in the level of the adoption of improved practices in agriculture. This point is of particular significance because it corroborates the role of 'functional literacy' in bringing about improvement in agricultural practices. The programme attracted a large number of farmers in the age group of 15-35 and the study further proved that the retention level is much higher in this group.

Thus the studies so far discussed were concerned with investigations into various types of efforts at educating adults.

As the coming of National Adult Education Programme in 1978 was regarded as a crucial landmark in the area of public policy, it was but natural that this programme would receive intense interest from analysts and students of public policy. Even more important is the fact that the policy makers themselves were keen on getting the implementation process evaluated for feed back purposes. As a matter of fact, the Union Ministry of Education and Social Welfare, itself identified six high powered research institutes for undertaking evaluation of the National Adult Education Programme.

These institutions are :

(1) Sardar Patel Institute of Economic and Social Research Ahmedabad, Gujarat.
(2) A.N. Sinha Institute of Social Sciences, Patna, Bihar.
(3) Indian Institute of Management, Ahmedabad, Gujarat.
(4) Tata Institute of Social Sciences, Bombay, Maharashtra
(5) Madras Institute of Development Studies, Madras, Tamil Nadu.
(6) Institute of Economic Growth, Delhi.

The studies conducted by these bodies obviously form an important part of our literature. It must be remembered that while we call these as official agencies, these are not official in the sense of being studies made by the very agencies that are implementing the National Adult Education Programme, but are studies undertaken by expert bodies invited by the policy sponsors to undertake critical evaluation. Except the Institute of Economic Growth, Delhi all other agencies have brought out their studies.

The second type of studies undertaken in the category are those conducted by individuals and organizations or other organizations and individuals. A rcview of evaluation studies undertaken by the agencies follows.

1. Sardar Patel Institute of Economic and Social Research, Ahmedabad

The Institute conducted a study on the Implementation of National Adult Eucation Programme in Gujarat. The study began in August 1978 and concluded in January 1979,

The main objective of the study was to make a quick appraisal of the adult education programme in terms of assessing the strengths and weaknesses of the programme and ascertaining the impact of the programme on the learners.

The sample of the study consisted of 45 voluntary agencies receiving financial assistance from Government of India to implement National Adult Education Programme. The total number of adult education centres that were selected through sampling are 181 which was 10 per cent of the total number of centres run through voluntary agencies. A total of 530 learners, 65 dropouts, 169 instructors were selected through stratified sampling method. The sample consists of 41 per cent male centres and 31 per cent female and 28 per cent, co-education centres. Of the total of 181 centres the study included separate centres for Scheduled Castes (18 per cent), Scheduled Tribes (5 per cent).

The average daily attendance in centres evalated was estimated at 25.3 (78 per cent). An interesting aspect here is that the report expressed doubt about the authenticity regarding attendance. It was reported that about 6.2 per cent of the adult education centres were closed before completing the 10 month period in Gujarat. Only 2 per cent of the enrolled adults were reported to have dropped out of the programme.

A heartening feature of the programme as stated in the appraisal report was that about 60 per cent of the learners in the sample acquired the skills of reading and writing.

The study curiously enough did not shed any light on the educational background of instructors except classification by sex. The report was also silent on the training of the instructors.

This study, the first appraisal of N A E P in Gujarat through voluntary agencies, offers many suggestions and recommendations. Some of the important recommendations include : (1) enhancement in instructor's honorarium (it was Rs. 50/- p.m. then), (2) increasing the participation of developmental departments and exchange of experiences between the voluntary agencies to increase the effectiveness of the programme.[46]

2. A.N. Sinha Institute of Social Sciences, Patna

An appraisal of the implemenlation of National Adult Education Programme in Bihar has been undertaken by the agency in 1979. It has selected 19 voluntary agencies for the study. The sample consists of 113 centres (10 per cent), 339 learners, 67 dropouts, and 113 instructors. The study did not include the potential learners and the elite. The sample consisted of larger number of male centres and a very small number of female centres. About 48 per cent of Adult Education Centres studied were exclusively meant for Scheduled Castes and 18 per cent for Scheduled Tribes. The average enrolment is reported to be 31.1. The percentage of Adult Education centres closed before completing 10 month duration was only 0.2. per cent.[47] The report, however, contains only partial data regarding the educational background of the instructors. About 58 per cent of the instructors underwent training for a period between 15—21 days and the remaining instructors received training for more than 21 days. The study brought out the various problems faced by voluntary agencies in locating centres, identifying learners, recruitment and training of instructors delay in getting the teaching materials as well as delay in release of grants to the voluntary agencies. The study offers many suggestions and recommendations. As most of these recommendations are, more or less, identical to those given by other studies under review, they would be discussed at the end of the reviews of these studies.

3. Indian Institute of Management, Ahmedabad

A study of the impact of the National Adult Education Programme in Rajasthan was taken up by the Indian Institute of Management, Ahmedabad. Seven voluntary agencies were selected for the study. The sample consists of 125 Adult Education Centres (10 per cent), 458 learners, 139 dropouts, 223 potential learners, 348 elites and 119 instructors. The break up of adult education centres by the Scheduled Caste and the Scheduled Tribes and other backward classes is 12.5 per cent, 20.8 per cent and 7.8 per cent respectively which comes to 41.1 per cent of the total number of Adult Education Centres. The average enrolment in each centre was reported as 27 and the average daily attendance was reported as 66.6 per cent. About 18 per cent of the Adult Education Centres were reported to have been closed before completion.

Further it revealed that a majority of instructors (56 per cent) studied up to middle school level. About 41 per cent of the instructors are matriculates and 3 per cent studied beyond matriculation. The study did not contain information regarding the distribution of instructors by their sex. Another omission of the study is about the training programme of instructors. A major finding of the study relates to learners' preference for education that was linked to functional aspects like agriculture, animal husbandry, poultry, credit facilities and other services. The study recommended greater involvement of developmental departments in the programme.

4. Second Appraisal

The Indian Institute of Management, Ahmedabad has also conducted a second appraisal with an enlarged sample which consisted of 50 voluntary Agencies, 186 Adult Education Centres, 768 learners, 321 dropouts, 464 potential learners, 555 elites and 184 instructors. Of the 186 centres selected 63 per cent are male centres, 31 percent female centres and the rest are mixed centres. It may be recalled here that the first appraisal did not give the division of Adult Education Centres by sex. The Scheduled Castes, the Scheduled Tribes and other backward class centres constitute about 9.6, 14.6 and 18.4 per centre respectively in the total sample.

The second appraisal recorded increase in the percentage of daily attendance at Adult Education Centres, however it did not give information about the closure of Adult Eduction Centres before the stipulated 10 month period. The educational status of the instructors in sample is that a majority (56 per cent) have middle school qualifications, 48 per cent fall between VIII and matriculation, and only 11 have above matric level qualification. The report is silent on the background of instructors, while it gave information about the distribution of the instructors by their sex (75 per cent male and 25 per cent female).

This appraisal too revealed that the National Adult Education Programme in Rajasthan was treated mainly as a literacy programme. Singificantly enough the study traced the main reason for neglect of functionality and social awareness components to lack of co-operation from developmental agencies of the government.

5. Tata Institute of Social Sciences, Bombay

The fifth important in this series is the one conducted by the Tata Institute of Social Sciences on the National Adult Education Programme in Maharashtra. The study did not confine itself to the role of the voluntary agencies alone. The Centres conducted by the Government agencies and Universities also figure in this study.

A total number of 292 centres was selected through the stratified random sampling method. The sample consists of 292 Adult Education Centres which constitute about 6 per cent of the sample. The data on various aspects of National Adult Education Programme is collected through an interview schedule administered to 1,102 learners, 232 dropouts, 249 potential learners and 292 instructors. About 58 per cent of the centres are male centres and 23 are female centres while combined centres account for only 5 per cent in the total sample. The break-up of centres by caste shows that 23 per cent of the Centres are exclusively opened for the Scheduled Castes, 17 per cent for the Scheduled Tribes, 9 per cent for other backward classes and the remaining 51 per cent for caste groups in the whole state. It was stated in the report that the enrolment in Maharashtra was slightly higher (30.9 per cent) than the recommended average enrolment of 30 learners per centre.

This appraisal revealed that on an average 6.4 persons per centre constituting 16.5 per cent of total enrolment dropped out before completing the programme. The sample consists of 17 per cent of the instructors with middle class educational background, 60 per cent between VIII and matriculation and 23 per cent above matriculation qualifications. Regarding the educational background the study shows that educational qualifications of instructors have a bearing on their performance. Delineating the caste structure, the report revealed that 24 per cent of the instructors belonged to Scheduled Caste and Scheduled Tribe categories. The appraisal pointed out the thin spread of training programme as it did not result in 100 per cent coverage of all instructors. Whereas the appraisal reports of Rajasthan, Gujarat and Tamil Nadu recorded the low priority given by voluntary Agencies owing to a host of reasons to functionality and social awareness components of National Adult Education Programme, the Maharashtra appraisal points out some attempts that had been made by some agencies to cover these two components.

One of the important findings of the report is that the infrastructural facilities available in villages were utilised effetively which was largely due to the success in co-ordination between various agencies involved.

6. Madras Institute of Development Studies

The Madras Institute of Development Studies undertook an evalution of Implementation of National Adult Education Programme in Tamil Nadu in 1980. A large sample (40 per cent) was drawn consisting of 31 voluntary agencies spread over 97 centres.

A total number of 194 learners, 85 dropouts, 97 potential learners and 97 instructors were interviewed with the help of schedules. An interesting feature of the adult education scene in Tamil Nadu is the existence of 54 per cent of female centres while the remaining 46 per cent are male centres. In rest of the states where appraisals were done, the situation was different. About 38 per cent of the total number of Adult Education centres are being run for the Scheduled Caste and the Scheduled Tribes categories. The study further revealed that on an average 21 adults are enrolled per centre and their attendance is 85 per cent which appears to be a little bit unrealistic considering the attendance reported in other appraisals. Nearly 17 per cent of the centres, according to the appraisal, have been closed before 10 months duration. The reason, as reported, was lack of interest on the part of the target group. The study estimated the rate of dropouts at 30 per cent.

The appraisal did not cover the educational background of the instructors and supervisors. A good percentage (67) of instructors belong to Scheduled Castes. As far as training of instructors was concerned, the report pointed ont that a few instructors underwent training very late after the commencement of the Adult Education Programme.

A bright spot of the National Adult Education Programme as revealed through the above appraisal was the co-operation received from community for the establishment of Adult Education Centres. A large number of Adult Education Centres were started in public places in villages. This is in sharp contrast to the position in Maharashtra where it was the goverment that had to provide space for the location of the study centres.

Summary

It can be seen from the review that except for the study by the Tata Institute of Social Sciences, Bombay, all the other five studies deal with programmes that were run exclusively by voluntary agencies. Each organization developed its own methodology. The objectives of these evaluation studies, as can be seen, are not very different from one another. The studies reveal a general satisfaction, with regard to the implementation of National Adult Education Programme through voluntary agencies. They have, however, brought out the inherent weaknesses of the programme. A general inadequacy of these studies may also be mentioned.

An examination of the socio-economic, educational, occupational status, and the commitment of the voluntary agencies to the programme would have certainly improved the depth of the two studies.

These studies have offered quite a number of suggestions. The Rajasthan appraisal recommended for an increase in the total budget allocation of this programme. Drawing the attention of the policy makers to the meagre sum of Rs 1704/- allotted to each learner, the report stated that while the government spends about 1 lakh rupees to educate a medical graduate, alottment of Rs 1704/-to educate an illiterate adult is ridiculously low.

Regarding the success of the National Adult Education Programme the appraisal conclusively observed that "about 15 to 18 adults per centre are definitely becoming literate. A few of them were found to be getting something more than literacy. They, however, belong to the economically deprived sections of the society".

The inadequacies with regard to the teaching material were touched upon by the Gujarat evaluation report. It was reported that nearly half of the instructors did not receive teaching material on functionality and social awareness. Thus the appraisal concluded that the instructors were not equipped properly to carry out the two vital components i. e. functionality and social awarenesses.[50]

Besides the Gujarat appraisal the other appraisals too referred to inadequacies in the supply of teaching learning material. Almost all reports recommended that (1) more teaching, learning materials should be provided to the Adult Education Centres, (2) more primers should be designed to cater to the interests and needs of heterogenous groups, (3) the material should be supplied in time, (4) the content of the material should be relevant to specific occupations of the learners.

Most of the studies also referred to problems relating to lack of proper seating arrangements for learners and inadequacy in lighting arrangements. As far as community participation is concerned, Tamil Nadu seemed to be the only exception, where the community facilities were voluntarily opened up to a majority of the centre. As has already been mentioned better co-ordination with the education department seems to be evident in the case of Maharashtra, for a mojority of centres were opened in the Schools. In any case, the involvement of the community seems to be marginal in the first year of the implementation of N A E P. The Rajasthan study showed that the villagers had helped initially in motivating the learners to join the adult education centres and some of them had even provided space for Adult Education Centres.

The survey of the evaluation studies is not exhaustive. The reports contain some suggestions relating to the policy behind the programme and vindicated their appraisal as a good feed back mechanism to the government. Some of the common features of the programme which have policy implications are :

(1) Preparation of more primers should be undertaken without delay keeping in view the varied and local needs of learners. Supplementary reading material for raising awareness of the learners should be made available to the learners. Steps should be taken to improve physical facilities like lighting. Regularity should be maintained in the supply of teaching/learning material.
(2) Effective follow-up and post literacy programme should

be organized to prevent the neo-literates from relapsing into illiteracy.

(3) Functional education component should be strengthened to satisfy the need of the learners who are interested in acquiring new skills for improving their earnings.

(4) Wide publicity should be given to various rural development programmes with a view to motivating prospective learners.

(5) Topics under social awareness should be increased especially those which concern them. Here the regional and socio-cultural variations should be kept in mind.

(6) The training programmes for adult education functionaries should be organised in such a manner that they enhance their understanding of NAEP as well as instill confidence in them.

(7) The delay in processing applications for financial assistance for adult education work by voluntary agencies must be cut down to the minimum.

(8) The project level committee should be activized.

(9) An increase in honorarium of the instructor need to be examined.

(10) The well established voluntary organisations at the national as well as state levels should be associated in the identification of new and emerging organisations.

Studies by 'Other' institutions

The second type of evaluation/appraisal studies on NAEP are by those organizations or agencies which were not initiated by the Government of India, Ministry of Education and Culture. Some of these are reviewed. Studies by individuals also follows.

The Xavier Labour Research Institute (XLRI)

The Xavier Labour Research Institute (XLRI) Jamshedpur, evaluated the impact of the National Adult Education Programme implemented by an agency based at Cuttack called the Jaua Kalyan Samithi. The agency received financial assistance for running NAEP in Koraput District of the state of Orissa in late 70's. The Xavier Labour Research Institute evaluated the impact of the programme on the clientele groups a year after the conclusion of the stipulated 10 month course. A total number of 30 Adult Education Centres was selected for the study. The sample consists of 155 learners (5 per cent), 30 dropouts (1 per cent) and 27 instructors. Among the total number of 3 centres selected 21 belong to the Scheduled Castes and the remaining are Adivasi and other categories.

The study showed that a majority (88 per cent) of the learners belong to agricultural labour. The educaitonal background of the learners families was also investigated and it was found that women in the age group of 15-35 formed a substantial section of illiterates. Eight per cent of the learners enrolled in adult education centres had been to a school before joining adult education centres which exhibits the shortcomings in the survey conducted for the purpose of identification of target group by the agency. On an average it was found that each learner in this category had spent two to five years in a school.

The reasons for dropping out of the formal education were stated as economic reasons and family pressures.

The report conveys that the learners have expressed satisfaction with the physical facilities available in the adult education centres. The perceptions of the adult illiterates about the benefits of joining adult education centres are as follows.

About 89 per cent of the learners stated that they joined the adult education centres only to acquire the ability to read and write. The agency to a large extent seems to have succeeded in its efforts to motivate illiterate adults to attend classes. About 53 learners stated that the instructors were quite helpful in rescuing them in their difficulties while about 47 per cent stated that they experienced difficulties in attending the classes.

The study rated 48 per cent of the sample as good at reading and 41 per cent as satisfactory in writing ability. In simple arithmatic 24 per cent of learners were categorised as good and 50 per cent as satisfactory. Thus, the overall performance in literacy has been described as fairly satisfactory in reading and simple arithmatic. The study indicated the need and scope for improvements.

As far as other components are concerned, the study reported that about 71 per cent of the learners reported that there was no increase in their income after they joined the adult education centres while 29 per cent said that there was an increase in their earnings, as a result of the participation in this programme. The study discovered that the functionality component of the programme needed better attention from the agency.

An analysis of the responses to the questions on social awareness component of the programme reveals the favourable reaction of learners to the advantages of family planning and to the benefits of savings. But, by and large, the learners were ignorant about minimum age for marriage, act on minimum wages, facilities available to farmers through such developmental agencies as S F D A etc. The study reported that majority of learners (59 per cent) did not know the minimum age for voting. Awareness about local problems such as drinking water, food and irrigation sources seem to be high among the learners though the capacity to solve the day to day problem is rated quite low. Some of the main difficulties experienced by learners as reported were: (a) lack of suitable study material (b) absence of trained instructors and (c) short duration of the programme. They suggested a strong follow up programme with greater emphasis on functionality component and supply of useful and relevant teaching material for the sources of the programme.

The situation with regard to the dropouts is more or less similar to other states as discussed earlier. In Orissa a a majority stated that they had discontinued owing to family problems. The incentives for their rejoining, as stated by them, were organizing cultural and entertainment programmes, introduction of monetary incentives etc.

The appraisal revealed that more than 90 per cent of the instructors have had no teaching experience. The training programmes organized by government and other voluntary agencies had reached only 48 per cent of the total instructors in the stage.

The failure to effectively implement the functionality and social awareness components of the N A E P were traced to lack of co-opertion from the development departments of the government. The study also reveals that the learners paid more attention to the lectures delivered by persons from outside. This observation is interesting as other appraisals have not focussed on this aspect.

The report referred to some of the weaknesses of the programme. These include, (1) lack of suitable study materials (2) lack of trained instructors and (3) short duration of the programme with no adequate follow up.

The report made several recommendations to increase the effectiveness of the programme. These include : (1) more attention to the training programmes of the instructors, (2) preparation of need-based curriculum, (3) increase in the number of female centres and (4) planning the post-literacy programme well in advance. The study thus covered almost all facets of N A E P and offered constructive suggestion.

Individual studies

An interesting study undertaken by Prof. G. Haragopal, Warangal district of Andhra Pradesh deserves mention here. Prof. Haragopal in his study[15] investigated the functioning of two Adult Education Centres—one consideren to be a successful centre and the other a failure. This study afforded an opportunity to examine the limited micro-level experience gained so far in the implementation of N A E P. This study also confirmed the partial achievement of tbe main components of the programme i.e. more emphasis on literacy component compared to the functionality and awareness of components. The reason for the success of Nagaram (a village in Warangal District) Adult Education Centres are (1) Readiness of the young person to invest their time as instructors, resources and energy for the cause, (2) their non-political image, (3) relative absence of factional fights in the area and (4) even while the curriculum was literacy-oriented', it took care to exclude what the inscructor termed as 'controversial issues.' In constrast to this, in Lambada Village an adult education centre was started for economically weaker sections. Initially the response was good but the enthusiasm faded over a period of time and generally attendance declined, finally culminating in the closure of the centre.

The causes for this development as investigated by the author were as follows : (1) Trooping of children into Adult Education Centres and view of the parents that education is for children and not for them. (2) The weak financial position of the spon sponsoring organizatiod which could not appoint a regular instructor. (3) The failure on the part of the instructor to converse in their language with the tribal learners. (4) The intervention of elections and the consequent diversion of interest from the programme and the general disinterest of the learners. The study further pointed out that centres were opened without proper planning. The study concluded that effective survey would have eliminated the crowding of children in one area.

Thus the study emphasises the need for comprehensive planning before starting adult education centres.

The studies by organisations sponsored by Government of India, studies by 'Other' organizations and individuals so far surveyed, provided the background for the present investigation The appraisal studies were done in respect of five states only. No exhaustive evaluation was done in other states particularly in states like Andhra Pradesh. The present study is a modest attempt to investigate the process of implementation and performance of National Adult Education Programme in Andhra Pradesh, one of the most backward states as far as literacy is concerned. But before an analysis of the implementation process is taken the institutional framework of the whole programme as conceived by policy makers is described which also provides a backdrop to the analysis that follows.

NOTES AND REFERENCES

1. Coleman, *Education and Political Development*. (New Jersey : Princeton University Press, 1965) p. ix.
2. See Plato's *Republic*.
3. See Aristotle's *Politics*.

4. John Dewey, *Democracy and Education*, (New Delhi : Light and Life Publishers, 1976) p. 20.
5. Report of the Education Commission, 1964-66, *Education and National Development*, (New Delhi : Ministry of Education and Culture, 1971) p. 9.
6. See Everett Reimer, *The School is Dead*, Ivan Illich, *De-Schooling Society*, John Holt, *Instead of Education : Ways to Help People To Do Better*, Paul Goodman, *Compulsory mis-education of Community of Scholars* (London : Penguine).
7. C.T. Kurien, *Educational Perspectives for Tamil Nadu* in Malcolm Adiseshiah (ed), Backdrop to the learning society' (Madras : Madras Institute of Development Studies, 1978) p. 25.
8. Bertrand Russel, *Education and Social Order* (London : George Allen and Unwin, 1971) p. 20.
9. Harold Silver, *Education and Social Condition* (London : Mathews, 1980) p. 19.
10. See T. W. Schultz, Reflection on Investment in Man, *Journal of Political Economy*, Vol. LXX, No. 5, Part 2, October 1962, pp. 1-8.
11. T.W. Schultz, *Investment in Human Capital in Poor Countries.*
12. *Summary Report of Organization for Economic Co-operation and Development* (O E C D), Washington, 1961, 'Policy Conference on Economic Growth and Investment in Education'. Quoted in James Coleman (ed) 'Education and Political Development' (New Jersey : Princeton University Press, 1965).
13. T.W. Schultz, *op. cit.*
14. V.K.R.V. Rao, Adult Education in India, *Indian Journal of Adult Education*, New Delhi, Vol. 34, October—December, 1976, p. 21.
15. See UNESCO, Paris, *Economic & Educational Aspects of Planning*, 1964.
16. Cippola, Carlo, M. *Literacy & Development in the West*, (London : Penguin, 1967) pp. 101-102.
17. *Ibid.*, p. 105. Also see Case Niehoff 'Educational Alternatives in National Development, Michigan, Institute of Internaltional Studies in Education, Michigan State University, 40-44.
18. Mc Clelland and D.G. Winter, *Motivating Economic Achievement* (New York : The Free Press, 1968), p. 31.
19. Strumlin, *Economics of Education in the U S S R* in Economic and Social Aspects of Educational Planning : UNESCO, Paris 1964, p. 72.
20. Harzog, A. William Jr. "Literacy and Community Economic Development in Rural Brazil", *Rural Sociology*, Vol.38, No. 3, 1973, p. 325.
21. Zilokowaski, J.A. "Illiteracy& Rural Economy", *The Ec nomic Times* (Annual 1973). p. 36.
22. Parolkar, J.S. "Education of Young Farmers and its impact on Agricultural Production", *Literacy Week*, Vol. No. 6, May 1972. pp. 58-62.
23. A.R. Desai and J.S. Parolkar, "The Relationship between Literacy

and Economic Productivity of Industrial Workers of Bombay : A Sociological Analysis", *Literacy Work* Vol. I No. 3, Summer, 1970, pp. 27-30

24. Mark Blaug, "*Economics of Education*", Geneva : International Labour Organization 1973, p. 32.
25. See Jenks. C. et. al. *Inequality*, (New York : Basic, 1972).
26 Arrow K.J. "Higher Education as a Tilter", *Journal of Public Economics* July 1973. Also see Berg, *Education and Jobs* : *The Great Training Robbery* (New York : Praeger, 1970).
27. Bowels, S and H. Gintis, *Schooling in Capitalist America*, (London : Routledge & Kegan Paul, 1971) p. 46.
28. Bourdien P. & J.C. Passeton, *Reproduction in Education* : *Society & Culture* (London : Sage Publishers, 1977) p. 50.
29. Bowman & Anderson, *Concurring the Role of Education* in Clifford Curtz (ed) "Old Societies and New States" (London : The Free Press, 1963) p. 248.
30. Chanchal Sarkar, "Missing the Boat in Population Policy", *Span*, April 1974.
31. Gopinath Nair P.R., Decline in Birth Rate in Kerala : A Hypothesis about the Inter-Relationship between Demographic Variables, Health Services & Education, *Economic & Political Weekly*, Vol. IX, 1974 p. 323.
32. *Ibid*., p. 333.
33. Paulo Frerie, *Pedagogy of the Oppressed*, (London : Penguine, 1972).
34. *Ibid.*, Foreword p. 9-14.
35. International Encyclopedia of Social Science (New York : Macmillan Co and The Free Press, 1972) p. 102.
36. Mohsini S.R. *Adult & Community Education* (New Delhi : Indian Adult Education Association, 1973).
37. J.P. Naik, *National Educational Policy 1947-77*, Pune Indian Institute of Education.
38. J.P. Naik, *The Education Commission and After*.
39. Agnihotri, *Evaluation of the Programme of Adult Education in Operation Under Pilot Plan in Wardha District* (Unpublished Ph.D. thesis) Nagpur, Nagpur University, pp. 42-89.
40. Johnson J.P. *A Proposal for the Establishment of a State-wide Adult Education Programme for Tamil Nadu*, Unpublished Ph.D. thesis, Madras University, 1970.
41. *Ibid.*
42. Planning Commission, Govt. of India, Programme Evaluation Organization, Report on the Working of Gram Sikhshan Mohim in Maharashtra, Government of India, Planning Commission Programme Evaluation Organization, New Delhi, 1965 p. 45.
43. Breggren, Corol & Lars, *The Literacy Process* : *A Practice in Domestication or Liberation* (London : Writers and Readers Publishing Co-Operative 1975) p. 49.

44. Venkataiah, N. *Impact of the FFLP on the Participants in A.P.* Unpublished Ph.D thesis) 1977, S.V. University, Tirupati.
45. Khan M.Z. *The Problem of Social (Adult) Education in four districts of Bombay and Mysore*, Dharwar, Unpublished Ph. D. thesis 1958, Karnataka, Dharwar.
46. N A E P in Gujarat (Ahmedabad :Sardar Patel Institute of Economic and Social Research, 1979) pp. 36-39.
47. *Adult Education for Development : A Study of N A E P in Bihar* (Patna : A.N. Sinha Institute of Social Studies, (1981) pp 169-179.
48. T.V. Rao, Anil Bhat and T.P. Rama Rao '*Adult Education For Social Change* (New Delhi, Manohar Publications, 1982) p. 62-67.
49. Rajasthan 66.6%, Gujarat 78%, Bihar 74%, Maharashtra 66%. According to MIDS report the high percentage of attendance may be ascribed to the advance information sent to Centres regarding their visit.
50. Atul Sharma, Vimal P. Shah, B.K. Parikh, National Adult Education Programme Gujarat—An Appraisal. Sardar Patel Institute of Economic and Social Research, Ahmedabad, 1979 p. 79-81.
51. Hargopal, G. "Literacy and Education', *Seminar*, 1979, pp. 30-34.

3

The Institutional Framework

In the late seventies the Government at the Union level attempted major policy changes in some spheres of public policy except perhaps in foreign policy. In pursuance of its election manifesto, a radical re-alignment of priorities was attempted within the education. For the first time since independence a National policy to educate illiterate adults was formulated to educate an estimated 100 million in the age group of 15-35 years. The target was fixed as 1983-84. The commitment of the government to adult education is reflected in Policy Statement on 'National Adult Education Programme' issued in 1978. It says "exclusion of a vast majority of the people from the process of education is a most disturbing aspect of educational and social planning. This has been uppermost in the consideration of the present government ever since it assumed office in March 1977".[2]

Recognising the role of primary education in checking illiteracy, the policy statement says that "while determined efforts must be made to universalise elementary education up to the age of 14 years, educational facilities must be extended to adult population to remedy their educational deprivation and to enable them to develop their potentiality. Indeed universalisation of elementary education and of adult literacy are mutually dependent".[3]

Further, the policy statement says that "the government have resolved to wage a clearly conceived well planned and relentless struggle against illiteracy to enable masses to play an active role in social and cultural change".[4]

Adult Education policy thus has been visualised as a major policy input to bring radical socio-economic and political changes. The report of the working group on adult education further confirms the government's intention on role of adult education as a 'change agent' when it says that : "Adult Education—looked upon as a method of human resource development, including literacy, functional development and creation of awareness among the poor regarding their inherent power to determine their destinies, should become the method in the new development process. It can contribute to the new development strategy in three significant ways : firstly, by making a substantial part of the work-force literate and better skilled ; secondly, by involvement of people in various developmental programmes which would make it possible to achieve optimum potential and minimize wastage ; and thirdly, by creation of awareness among the poor regarding the laws and policies of government, whereby, it would be possible to implement the strategy of re-distributive justice".[5]

Touching on the various aspects of the problem of illiteracy the policy statement clearly stated that "a massive programme should be launched to cover the vast segment of population in the 15-35 age group as early as possible".[6] The planners of this programme dwelt at length on the organizational aspects of the National Adult Education Programme.

The role of non-governmental and semi-government agencies in the implementation of this programme was particularly recognised.

In fact, the policy document makes it very clear that "Adult Education must cease to be a concern only of the educational authority. It should be an indispensable input in all (major) sectors of development, particularly where participation of the beneficiaries is crucial to the fulfilment of development objectives".[7] Further it was stated that "A pre-requisite of an adult education movement is that all agencies ; government, voluntary, private and public sector industry, institutes of formal education should lend strength to it".[8] Thus it can be seen that the policy planners rightly perceived the importance of non-governmental agencies (popularly known as NGO's) in the implementation of qualitative public policy like adult education.

A unique feature of the National Adult Education Programme is the special place given to voluntary agencies. The policy statement emphatically stated that "voluntary agencies have a special role to play and necessary steps shall have to be taken to secure their full involvement".[9]

Thus the goal liquidating illiteracy in the country through a National Adult Education Programme is being planned and this programme was launched in 1978 throughout the country on Mahatma Gandhi's birth anniversary. It was planned to cover 100 million illiterates in the 15-3 age group within five years. The following table gives year wise phasing of the programme.

TABLE 6

Target Fixed For the Coverage of Adult Illiterates Under N A E P

Year	Annual coverage	Cumulative coverage
1978-79	1.5	1.5
1979-80	4.5	6.0
1980-81	9.0	15.0
1981-82	18.0	33.0
1982-83	32.0	65.0
1983-84	35.0	100.0

Source : Government of India, Ministry of Education and Culture, Policy statement on National Adult Education Programme and N A E P—an outline. pp. 18-19.

Establishment of National Board of Adult Education

It may be recalled that the National Adult Education Programme was started as a result of the initiative taken by the then Union Government which was elected to power in late 70's. The preliminary work relating to the programme began with the establishment of a National Board of Adult Education[10] in 1977. The Chairman of the Board was Shri Morarji Desai who was the Prime Minister then. The composition of the board includes some ministers of Central Government, a Minister dealing with adult education from each of the regions of the country, heads of organizations such as University Grants Commission, Central Social Welfare Board, Khadi and Village Industries Corporation, Federation of Indian Chambers of Commerce and Industry, Indian Adult Education Association and a host of other non-officials and field workers.

The National Board of Adult Education has set up five committees to attend to specific tasks relating to adult education programme. These were :

1. The Committee on Preparatory action.
2. The Committee on Motivation.
3. Committee on Voluntary Agencies.
4. Committee on Post-literacy and follow-up.
5, Committee on Evaluation.

It was stated in one of the publications of the Ministry of Education and Social Welfare that "all important decisions taken by various committees are generally endorsed by the National Board of Adult Education".[11]

National Level : The National Board of Adult Education (NBAE)

The overall responsibility for the administration of the national adult education grogramme rests with the Ministry of Education (now rechristened as Ministry of Human Resource Development). It provides secretariat to the National Board of Adult Education. The Ministry also deals with the various inter-ministerial matters and is charged with the responsibility of overseeing the implementation of National Adult Education Programmes in various states. The schemes of assistance to voluntary agencies and Shramik Vidyapeeths under the Ministry directly sanctions grants and is thus administered by the Central Ministry.

The organisational chart drawn here gives a picture of the administrative framework of the National Adult Education Programme.

As can be observed from the chart, the programme is being planned to be implemented through a variety of governmental, semi-governmental and non-governmental agencies.

The administrative structure for the programme extends from the central to the field level (i.e. Adult Education Centre). At the Central level, as has already been discussed, the Ministry of Education and the Central Directorate of Adult Education are in the overall in-charge of the programme management. The Ministry and the Directorate have a special responsibility, for involvement of various organizations like voluntary agencies universities and colleges. The specific functions of the Directorate include : (a) arrangement of training programmes ; (b) production of teaching/learning material ; and (c) evaluation. These two agencies are also charged with the responsibility of involving other developmental ministries like Agriculture Rural development and other autonomous agencies in the programme. In 1987 the programme has been re-designated as National Literacy Mission and target year had been put off to the year 2020.

At the state level, the State Board of Adult Education (S B A E) is regarded as an apex body for entire state. It is usually chaired by the State's Chief Mintster or the Education Minister. The main functions of the Board are : (a) to provide policy guidelines ; (b) creating a favourable environment ; and (c) reviewing the progress of the programme.

A Steering Committee to aid and advise the state board of Adult Education is also created with such functions like working out implementation strategies like location of centres, target of coverage as well as co-ordination of the programme besides involving other developmental departments. Further this agency is also expected to take steps to involve government, semi-governmental and voluntary agencies and the implemen-

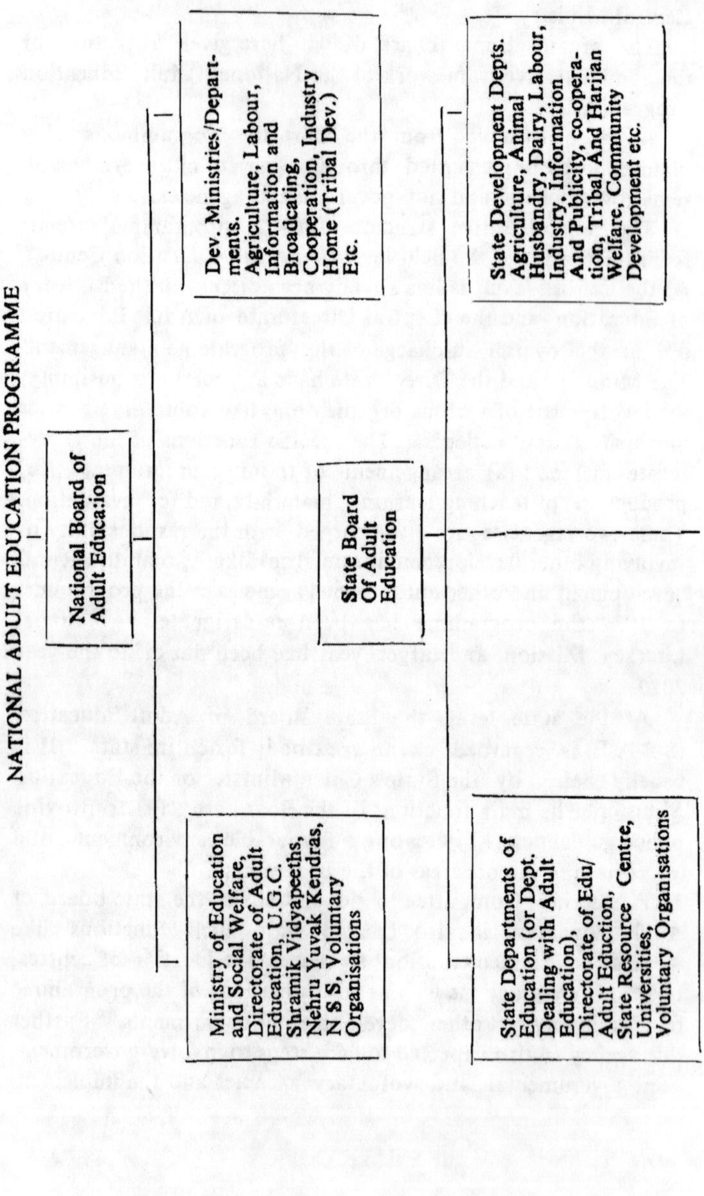
NATIONAL ADULT EDUCATION PROGRAMME
National Board of Adult Education
Ministry of Education and Social Welfare, Directorate of Adult Education, U.G.C. Shramik Vidyapeeths, Nehru Yuvak Kendras, N S S, Voluntary Organisations
Dev. Ministries/Departments. Agriculture, Labour, Information and Broadcasting, Cooperation, Industry Home (Tribal Dev.) Etc.
State Board Of Adult Education
State Departments of Education (or Dept. Dealing with Adult Education), Directorate of Edu/Adult Eduction, State Resource Centre, Universities, Voluntary Organisations
State Development Depts. Agriculture, Animal Husbandry, Dairy, Labour, Industry, Information And Publicity, co-operation, Tribal And Harijan Welfare, Community Development etc.

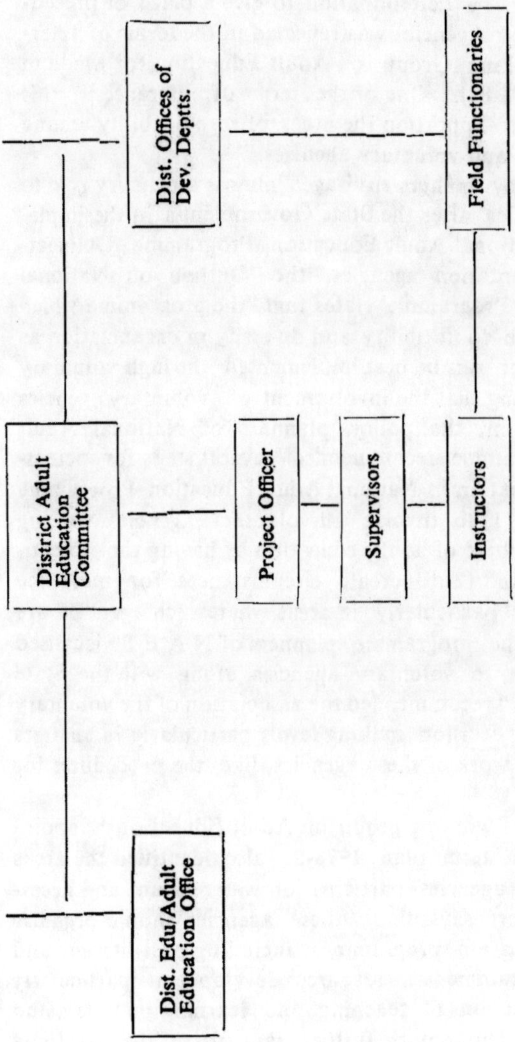

Source : Summary of the Report of the Working Group of Adult Education for Mediam Term Plan 1978-83 to 85.

tation. Monitoring of the progress of the programme is yet another task entrusted to the Steering Committee.

The government's determination to give a place of precedence to Voluntary Agencies was reflected in the terms of reference of the Working Group on Adult Education for Medium Term Plan (1978-83). One of the term of reference to this committee was "to apportion the areas of responsibility among the centre, states and voluntary agencies."[12]

Thus the policy makers envisaged almost a primary role to voluntary agencies after the State Government's in the implementation of National Adult Education Programme. Delineating on implementation agencies, the 'Outline on National Adult Education Programme' states that "the programme which gives importance to flexibility and diversity in organization as well as its content can be best implemented through voluntary agencies."[13] Noting that the involvement of voluntary agencies is not much then, the policy planners of National Adult Education Programme recommended several steps for increasing their participation in National Adult Education Programme which include : (1) to involve all voluntary agencies working at present in the field of adult education or having the potentiality to do so ; and (2) to create circumstances for emergence of new agencies, particularly in areas where such agencies are few. Further, the programme planners of N A E P visualised partnership role to voluntary agencies along with the State Governments and recommended the association of the voluntary agencies at all decision making levels particularly in matters which affect the work of these agencies, like the procedures for applying grants.

The report of working group on Adult Education[14] appointed for medium term plan 1978-83 also identified the areas where voluntary agencies' participation was relevant and necessary. The report says that "these agencies should organise field adult education programmes, including post-literacy and follow-up programmes . . . resource development particularly training, production of teaching and learning materials and evaluation."[15] The report further says that "the all India voluntary organizations should be encouraged to organize orientation programmes for other voluntary agencies."[16] Commenting on the rigid procedures in government which may drive away the enthusiastic agencies from the programme the working group recommended that "the government must also replace the mechanism which obstruct involvement of the voluntary agencies by enabling mechanisms."[17] However, the group struck a note of caution regarding the selection of voluntary agencies in the implementation of N A E P and recommended that only those agencies should be selected for financial assistance which have potentiality to implement the programme.

The functional agency of the State Government for implementation of National Adult Education Programme is the Directorate of Adult Education,[18] with specific tasks such as : (1) preparation of plans ; (2) encouraging voluntary agencies to participate ; (3) direction and overall supervision of government programmes ; (4) overseeing and co-ordination of programmes taken up by various agencies other than the government ; (5) selection and placement of personnel ; and (6) monitoring and evaluation of the programme.

The next important agency in the Nation Adult Educational Programme is the State Resources Centre which is entrusted with such essential functions as : (1) preparation of teaching/learning material ; (2) organization of seminars ; (3) development of methodological guidelines for curriculum preparation ; and (4) training support to the programme, including post-literacy programmes, evaluation, research and publications.

District Level

At the district level the major responsibility for the implementation of National Adult Education Programme is vested with the District Collector. He/She occupies this position as the Chairman of District adult education board/commtitee. The government projects are expected to be supervised by the District Collector who would organize, co-ordinate and supervise the implementation of National Adult Education Programme through all agencies—governmental, voluntary and other agencies at the district level. The Collector is assisted by the District Adult Education Officer, now styled as Dy.

Director of Adult Education in Andhra Pradesh. The District Adult Education Officer/Deputy Director of Adult Education acts as member secretary of the District Adult Education Committee/Board which first of all scrutinises the proposals for starting Adult Education Programme in the district. All the government project officers and some representatives of voluntary agencies, Universities, Nehru Yuvak Kendras are members of this committee. The committee is also charged with an important responsibility of processing the applications of voluntary agencies for financial assistance and also to assess progress of their work periodically. Besides, tha district adult education committee also monitors and evaluates the work of all agencies in their jurisdiction.

Project Level

A key unit for planning and implementation of national adult education programme is a project which usually consists of about 300 adult education centres. It is headed by a Project Officer. He/She is assisted by an Assistant Project Officer. In Andhra Pradesh the geographical area of a project generally is co-terminus with that of a block. (Block has been further divided into Mandals recently). A project in National Adult Education Programme framework is visualised as an autonomous unit with Project Officer vested with powers to run administration, to manage finances, appointment and training of instructors and supervisors (which was since passed on to State Resources Centre) taking steps to prepare the teaching/learning materials and finally organize post-literacy and other follow up activities.

For every 30 Adult Education Centres in a project, a supervisor is appointed who is expected to assist the Project Officer in resource development particularly in training instructors. Besides these functions the supervisors discharge such varied functions like liaison with development functionaries, Mahila Mandals, ensuring regular supply of teaching/learning materials and payment of honorarium to instructor, and in organizing post literacy operations.

Centre Level

The critical unit of the administration in the organisational framework of National Adult Education Programme is the adult education centre under the charge of an instructor. The instructor's main functions, besides teaching, are : (a) Survey ; (b) ensuring co-operation with village level developmental functionaries ; (c) establishment of rapport with village elites and sending periodical reports about the progress of the programme.

Thus, it can be seen that a vast administrative machinery at various levels was created to Implement National Adult Education Programme. The National Board of Adult Education, The State Boards, Steering Committees, the Project Level Committees are expected to function as Co-ordinating bodies.

Instructional Cadre

The policy planners of National Adult Education Programme have identified six categories of people as the, 'instructional cadre'.[19] They include : (1) The School teachers; (2) Students ; (3) Village youths ; (4) Ex-serviceman and other retired personnel ; (5) Field level grovernment and other functionaries and (6) Voluntary social workers.

School teachers in particular were regarded as the catchment area to take up the job of instruction in adult education centres. The students, as part of the National Service Scheme activities, were marked as another source.

The policy planners also gave a place to the village youth with some educational background in running the adult education centres. With an expectation that the retired people would be free and would accept a job which would yield a supplemental income to them, ex-servicemen and retired persons are identified as one of the sources for the teaching part of the programme. The village level workers and Gram Sevikas and voluntary social workers are yet another category who were identified for the job of instructors.

Resource Development

The conceptual position spelt out in the policy statement[20] implies creation and development of a resource base for National Adult Education Programme, the priority being given to diversified and need based learning material. The National Resource group consists of such agencies like the Central Directorate of Adult Education, various other agencies of Central Government and National level voluntary agencies.

The next important unit in resource development is the State Resources Centres (SRC's) which in co-operation with the National Resource Group and by continuous interaction with the field, are expected to attend to the task of resource development. Some of the important functions of the SRC's include: (a) development of competence in curriculum planning and development ; (b) preparation of diversified teaching/learning material to suit the learners' needs ; and (c) organization of training programmes to key level functionaries.

Financial Arrangement

An amount of Rs. 200 crores had been allocated to this programme in the draft sixth five year plan (1978-83)[21] by the then Janata Government.[22] To cover 65 million adult illiterates the cost was estimated at about Rs. 686 crores. The following table gives the details of the year wise expenditure outlay for N A E P from 1978-1983. Recently the Union government announced that a 'National Literacy Mission' (NLM) to educate about 80 million adult illiterates would be implemented from 1987-88. The cost of the programme was stated to be Rs. 550 crores. It has been calculated then

TABLE 9

Year-wise Expenditure outlay

(in crores of rupees)

Year	Cost
1978-79	15.84
1979-80	48.52
1980-81	95.04
1981-82	190.05
1982-83	336.95
Total cost	686.40

Source : N A E P *Medium Term Plan*, Government of India, Ministry of Education and Culture, 1978.

that the cost for 'educating' an adult illiterate would be Rs. 60 per year. Since the programme planners expected that one third of the participants would dropout the cost per learner was worked out as Rs. 90/-.

It was also expected that some funds would be available in the form of contributions and the final cost per learner was put at Rs. 80/—. This estimate, however, does not include expenditure on administrative structure and other activities connected with the programme.

Summary

An impressive administrative structure seemed to have been provided at national, state and district levels to implement the N A E P. A number of state governments have created separate directorate of Adult Education. The State government send their proposals to the Ministry for starting projects. The Central Directorate is also associated in scrutinising such proposals. A set of guidelines were formulated which facilitate easy scrutiny of the proposals. Projects sponsored and entirely funded by the Central Government are known as Rural Functional Literacy Programme's (R F L P), projects funded by states are known as 'State Adult Eduction Programme's (S A E P's). The Central Ministry of Education directly sanctions the grants to voluntary agencies for running adult education programme. The State Governments are expected to be informed about the sanction of grants sanctioned to voluntary agencies by the Government of India and the state directorates are supposed to supervise the implementation by the voluntary agencies. However, like in any programme we notice snags in the organisational design. In the earlier years of the programme some voluntary agencies got the financial sanction bypassing the State Governments, the Directorates of Adult Education and District Adult Education Committees using the political linkages they had with the power structure at the union level. Such situations gave rise to infiltration of undesirable elements into the programme. Monitoring of N A E P is stated as an important component of programme management.[24] Elaborate procedures have been evolved to monitor the progress.

It was stated in one of the handouts released by the Central Directorate of Adult Education, that qualitative reporting is desirable rather than reporting of mere quantitative data. One of the aspects of the reporting procedure is a column relating to the achievement of learners in terms of the main objectives of the programme viz., literacy, functionality and social awareness. However, except in the year 1979-80 we do not find it in the annual report brought out by either the Ministry of Education or the Central Directorate of Adult Education in the subsequent years.

The States are not coming forward to take up the programme on the scale expected.[25] For the last five years the Central Government's share is very much higher compared with the other agencies.[26]

Coming to the personnel policies, most of the staff of State Directorates are brought on deputation. The discussions with some officials revealed that the staff lacked the required commitment that is so necessary for the success of the programme.[27] The visits by them to the 'Centres' either under the R F L P, or S A E P or by Voluntary Agencies is routine and their reactions to the problems is passive.[28] Thus the personnel policy with regard to the State Directorates warrants reconsideration.

While about twelve Deputy Directors at the rate of one for every two districts are required for effective supervision of the programme, there are about four or five Deputy Directors which indicates absence of commitment on the part of the State of Andhra Pradesh. The supervisory recruitment policy was marked by ad-hocism and short sightedness.[29] It is to be noticed that there is a lot of gap between what policy planners visualised and what is actually happening now in the States. The point is that since the over-all management of both centrally sponsored and other agencies programmes rests with the State Governments, the Education Department of the State and the Directorate of Adult Education needs to be properly equipped in terms of staff and other requirements.

Coming to the District level administrative framework, the much burdened District Collector is further loaded with the Chairmanship of the District Adult Education Committee in which besides District Education Officer and Deputy Director of Adult Education the voluntary agencies participating in the programme, are also members. Most of the District level Education Committees are inactive for one reason or the other. Curiously enough, the Andhra Pradesh State Government made the District Education Officer the Convenor of the District Adult Education Committee. While the field representative of the Directorate of Adult Education is just a member. In this superior subordinate power relationship sometimes a junior District Educational Officer may act as a boss to the senior Deputy Director of Adult Education.[30] The power conflict between them may have an adverse effect on the effectiveness of the programme.

As already pointed out the National Board of Adult Education (N B A E) is not meeting regularly to give a higher and necessary policy direction. This has sometimes created vacuum in policy making. Even the meetings of State Boards of Adult Education and the State level Steering Committees are not held regularly as they are expected to. With the result a clearly conceived policy on Adult Education is suffering from ad-hocism. The progress of the programme in terms of number of adult education centres opened from 1979-80 to 1983-84 for whole country can be gleaned from Table 10.

Data in Table 10 presents the progress in terms of number of adult education centres opened and functioning in the country from 1979-80 to 1983-84. Reporting procedures seemed to have been modified since 1984-85. It was given to understand that the monitoring of the progress gradually became ineffective. The central directorate of adult education is not supplied information by its counterparts in the states. We only find number of projects (each project consists of 300 ABC's) sanctioned by the Union Government. That is the reason why data is not up to date.

From the table it will be clear that the majority of centres are run under centrally sponsored functional literacy projects followed by the States. Contrary to the popular expectations and policy statements, the role of voluntary agencies in the programme appears to be declining. This may be due to the

TABLE 10

Total Number of Adult Education Centres Opened

Sl. No.	Name of Scheme	1979-80	1980-81	1981-82	1982-83	1983-84
1.	Rural Functional Literacy Programme	28,996 (35.56)	37,643 (41.44)	48,369 (52.55)	63,602 (49.55)	99,574 (59.01)
2.	State Adult Education Programme	19,644 (24.1)	38,178 (41.72)	37,352 (40.58)	59,840 (46.62)	59,015 (34.97)
3.	Voluntary Agencies	19,029 (23.34)	11,293 (12.34)	339 (.36)	822 (.64)	5,873 (3.48)
4.	Nehru Yuvak Kendras	7,129 (8.74)	1,514 (1.65)	4,884 (5.31)	1,519 (1.1835)	527 (0.3)
5.	Universities & Colleges	3,684 (3.91)	2,340 (2.56)	585 (.64)	899 (.69)	644 (0.381)
6.	Others	3,049 (3.74)	542 (.59)	516 (.50)	1,662 (1.3)	,0837 (1.83)
	Total	81,531	91,510	92,045	1,28,344	1,68,720

Source : Annual Reports (Figures in parentheses indicate percentages)
Ministry of Education, Government of India.

mounting criticism against the particiption of voluntary sector as it was alleged in Parliament and Press that some agencies are diverting funds earmarked for adult education to 'other' purposes. The Committee headed by Prof. D.S. Kothari appointed to review the Nationat Adult Education Policy, however, gave a clean chit to voluntary agencies,

The role of Nehru Yuvak Kendras, Universities & Colleges and others also shows a decline. National Adult Education Policy appears to be almost under an eclipse for two years i.e., between 1980-81 and 81-82. The report of the review Committee on National Adult Education Policy had been withheld. The whole programme was in a state of suspended animation till 1982.

The New Education Policy—1986 mentions continuing priority to adult education. The document on 'Programme of Action' too delineates on various ways and means to stir activity on the adult education front. In 1987, the Union Government announced a National Literacy Mission to educate about 80 million adult illiterates in the age group of 15-35 years by 1995. Thirty million are proposed to be brought under the programme by 1990. It should be remembered that this is the second time the Government changed the target year.

Changes in the institutional framework are on cards. The Union Directorate of Adult Education is proposed to be converted into a National Resource Centre. A high power board seems to be in the offing to give a new thrust to the programme.

The process of implementation of National Adult Education Programme is attempted in the next chapter starting with an analysis of the instructional cadre.

NOTES & REFERENCES

1. *Policy Statement on National Adult Education Programme,* (NAEP), Government of India, Ministry of Education and Social Welfare, 1978, New Delhi, p. 2.
2. *Ibid*, p. 2.
3. *Ibid*, p. 3.
4. *Ibid*, p. 3.

5. Summary of the Report of the Working Group on Adult Education for Medium Term Plan, 1978-83, Government of India, Ministry of Education and Social Welfare, New Delhi, 1978, p. 3.
6. Policy Statement on NAEP, *op. cit.* p. 3.
7. *Ibid*, p. 3.
8. *Ibid*, p. 3.
9. *Ibid*. p. 3.
10. NAEP : *An Outline*, Government of India, Ministry of Education and Social Welfare, New Delhi, 1978, p. 8.
11. *Ibid*, p. 9.
12. Summary of the Report of the Working Group on Adult Education for Medium Term Plan, 1978-83, *op. cit.* p. 21.
13. NAEP : *An Outline*, Ministry of Education and Social Work, *op. cit.* p. 12.
14. Report of the Working Group on Adult Education for Medium Term Plan 1978-83, *op. cit.* p. 12.
15. *Ibid*, p. 12.
16. *Ibid*, p. 12.
17. *Ibid*, p. 13.
18. NAEP : *An Outline, op. cit.* p. 14.
19. *Ibid*, p. 16.
20. *Ibid*, p. 18, Also see *Policy Statement on NAEP*, p. 1.
21. The Janata Government had allocated about Rs. 200 crores in the Draft Sixth Five Year Plan for 1978-83. It was reduced to Rs. 128 crores by the Congress-I Government in Sixth Plan for 1980-85. The Congress-I Government had put off the target year to 1995. A national literacy mission with an outlay of Rs. 550 crores is proposed to be implemented. See *The Hindu*, August 1987.
22. *Draft Sixth Five Year Plan, 1978-83*, Planning Commission, Government of India, Ministry of Planning, New Delhi, 1978, p. 43.
23. NAEP : *An Outline op. cit.* p. 9.
24. *Monitoring National Adult Education Programme*, Directorate of Adult Education, Ministry of Education & Social Welfare, New Delhi, 1978, p. 9.
25. See The *Statesman*, New Delhi, November 4, 1979 and *Indian Express*, Hyderabad, February 13, 1983.
26. The financial arrangement of the programme is that the matching grants are provided by the Central Government under Rural Functional Literacy Programme to the States to supplement their efforts. But the projects sponsored by the Central Government are always higher than the states.
27. The Supervisor of a Government Project remarked that most of the deputationists continue to carry their parent department culture. In his opinion the greatest damage was from those deputationists who rarely bothered to work with commitment.
28. The response from them is particularly disturbing as a good number

of them seemed to have joined new jobs thinking that provides relief to them. Moreover it takes fairly long time for them to get over their bureaucratic culture. The adult education work demands different style of functioning.

29. The government cancelled written test and interviews for the post of supervisors when allegations of leakage of question papers were made in 1982-83. The High Court stayed the selection later. The point is that on both occasions the government as well as the State Directorate of Adult Education do not seem to have anticipated such contingencies like leakage of question papers. This short sightedness led to doubts about the legitimacy of the selection process.
30. The Deputy Director of Adult Education attends to regular work concering the programme in his zone (A zone consists of 2 districts). The District Education Officer is made the convenor of the District Adult Education Committee. In some areas the DEOs are juniors to the Dy. Directors. The relationship is often marked by conflict for power. The meetings of the District Adult Education Committees when convened were postponed on a few occasions without valid reasons. When the investigator probed it was revealed that Dy. Director it seems felt insulted when a junior officer tried to boss over him. All this shows how the administrative culture internalized by the administrators will have an adverse effect on the smooth running of an important programme.
31. The figures are collected from the various annual reports of the Central Education Ministry from 1979-80 to 1983-84.
32. Various reasons are cited for the decreasing role of the voluntary Agencies in NAEP. Most important is the suspicion of the present Government that the Voluntary Agencies with their political leanings may misuse the funds. The review Committee appointed to go into all aspects of NAEP in 1979 strongly recommended increased involvement of the Voluntary Agencies. This report itself was put in cold storage for nearly two years. The word 'National' was dropped from the title of the programme. It is now referred as AEP with reduced priority. Applications from Voluntary Agencies are throughly screened before being admitted for grants-in-aid. Some agencies vexed up with the attitude of the Government and abandoned the idea of running programme with the aid from the government. *The Programme of Action—87* refers to adult education programme as National Programme of Adult Education (NPAE). See the POA pp. 130-134 ; 1987, Government of India.

4

The Implementation : Instructors and Supervisors

In the previous chapter the institutional framework of the National Adult Educational Programme as visualised by policy makers is described. The functions of the each administrative unit of the programme are given i.e. at the central level, the National Board of Adult Education, the Central Ministry of Education, The Central Directorate of Adult Education; at the state level the State Board (s) of Adult Education, the State Steering Committees, the State Ministry of Education, the State Directorate of Adult Education; at the District level, the District Adult Education Committee headed by the District Collector,the Office of the Deputy Director of Adult Education and finally at the block level the office of the project officer assisted by Supervisors.

Implementation Agencies

It may be worthwhile to recall here that the programme is being implemented through five types of agencies (1) the State Governments, (2) the Voluntary Agencies, (3) the Universities and Colleges through their Adult Education and National

Service Schemes (NSS), (4) the Nehru Yuvak Kendras and finally (5) through the Integrated Child Development Schemes of the Women and Child Welfare Directorate of the State Governments. A variety of organizations, Governmental, semi-governmental and non-governmental thus, are associated for the first time in the implementation of National Adult Education Programme on a massive scale. The policy statement on National Adult Education Programme clearly spelt out the arrangements that have to be made to administer the progrrmme. Delineating on the organizational issues, the policy statement says that "from the organisational point of view it is of utmost importance that elaborate preparations are made before launching this massive programme. It is of greatest importance that implementation of adult education programme is decentralized".[1] The policy of associating multiplicity of organization i.e. governmental, semi-governmental and non-governmental raises a number of administrative problems like co-ordination which is considered as one of the key problems.

Once the goals of the programme have been set, its plans and policies determined, money provided, organization tailored to the need, personnel assigned, directions given, delegations determined and supervision provided for, then the co-ordination is the means of bringing all those factors together in an inter-locking relationship. Co-ordination has further been viewed as a means by which a blend is secured.[2]

There are a few generalizations which are usually attributed to the principle of co-ordination.

1. The more the work of a bureaucracy is sub-divided, the more important it is that the components be assembled in a unified relationship, if the goal of the programme is to be achieved.

2. Co-ordination relies on the authority that accompanies hierarchy and position, it relies also on individual competence, understanding and voluntary co-operation.

(3) The better the goals of the programme are understood and accepted by those who work for it the easier it is to secure voluntary co-operation.

4. Even when conditions evoke voluntary co-operation, co-

ordination is difficult because people in a bureaucracy tend to have a natural desire to be left alone. Consequently, the application of the techinques of co-ordination is time consuming responsibility of the executive and becomes more so as he (The Executive) rises in the hierarchy.

5. Relatively more time is spent on external co-ordination than internal co-ordination.

Administration therefore is an attempt to bring diverse units into a working relationship so that, together, they result in achieving the goal. Co-ordination is viewed as placing the many aspects of an enterprise in proper position relative to each other and to the programme of which they are a part of the policy. In other words, it harmoniously combines 'agents' and 'functions' towards the achievement of a desired goal.[3]

According to professor Mohit Bhattacharya, Co-ordination assumes importance in organization theory in the context of "intra-organizational interdependencies. Situations of interdependence have to be objectively identified within the organization".[4] Discussing the various aspects of co-ordination, the author wrote that "co-ordination is a process of harmonisation of the activities of the different parts of an organization with a view to achieving the the goals of an organization".[5]

Keeping in view the above theoretical premise on the principle of co-ordination an attempt is made in this chapter to study how co-ordination is secured by the agencies which have run the programme. As the implementation of the programme forms chief concern of the investigator, it is proposed to analyse the problems involved in the following order.

1. The instructors, method of their recruitment, perceptions about the centres, curriculum and learners.

2. The views of the supervisory staff, those of the agencies on the one hand and of the governmental departments on the other about running of the centres (constraints and limitation), instructional material and instructors, mutual perceptions between the two branches of the supervisory cadres to highlight problems of co-ordination.

3. Structures and functions of the agencies, the opinions of the office bearers and other concerned about the programme and particularly their views on the government's role in organi-

sing the programme through the agencies, the problem of co-ordination inter-se the governmental bodies connected in promoting voluntary agencies in he programme and the agencies themselves, will be highlighted.

1. Instructors' method of recruitment, perceptions about centres, curriculum and the learncrs

Instructors or organizers of Animaters of an adult education centre is virtually the king-pin in the entire administrative edifice of Adult Education Programme. The policy outline on National Adult Education Programme states that 'the governing consideration in assigning responsibility for instructional arrangements should be (a) the suitability of the persons concerned to organize programmes with a grasp of the conceptual standpoint and with a spirit of commitment'[6].

Further the policy planners have identified school teachers, students, village/youth, ex-servicemen and others including retired personnel as the main reservoir from which the instructional cadre can be drawn.

The policy statement as well as the subsequent documents relating to the National Adult Education Programme however have not dealt much with the methods or procedures for recruitment to the posts of instructors and thus seems to have left enough autonomy to the agencies in selecting the instructors.

One hardly needs to emphasise the point that the selection procedures adopted by the implementing agencies to recruit instructors would go a long way in ensuring the success of the Adult Education Programme.

In this section it is proposed to examine the methods of recruitment of instructors adopted by the agencies in the sample. The following table presents the methods followed by different agencies in the recruitment of instructors.

As can be seen from the table the broad methods of selection of instructor adopted by the agencies in the sample are (1) Interview, (2) Personal contact, (3) Approach by the agency (4) village committees' recommendation.

TABLE 11

Method of Selection of Instructors

Sl. No.	Agency	Interview	Personal contact	Approach by Agency	Village Committee recommended	Total
1.	Andhra Mahila Sabha (AMS)	—	8	2	—	10
2.	Bhagavathula Charitable Trust (BCT)	3	—	—	—	3
3.	Comprehensive Rural Operations Service Society, (CROSS)	—	—	1	2	3
4.	Durga Sangh Seva Samaj (DSS)	3	—	—	—	3
	Total	6	8	3	2	19 (100.00)

The method of selection of instructors through interview was followed by only two agencies in the sample. Each of these agencies has given wide publicity to the programme and this has attracted quite a few applicants for the posts of instructors. While the Bhagavathula Charitable Trus (BCT) did not specify preference in selection to the instructors posts, the Durga Sangh Seva Samja (DSS) specified that it would give preference to the teachers, retired or in service. About 50 applications are said to have been received for 30 posts of instructors in the case of Bhagavathula Charitable Ttust. The selection committee of this agency consisted of the project officer, Director of Adult Education, Andhra University (Visakhapatnam) and its own officials in charge of horticulture besides block level official in-charge of agriculture and education. All the three instructors in the sample reported that they were inerviewed on such wide-ranging issues like problem of illiteracy, economic development, poverty etc.

The Durga Sangh Seva Samaj also received around 50 applications for the post of instructors out of which 30 were selected. As has already been mentioned, the agency gave preference to teachers, retired as well as those in service. The selection committee constituted by this agency included the Project Officer, the supervisor, block level official incharge of education. The candidates were examined on general topics.

Coming to other agencies, the Andhra Mahila Sabha did not seem to have followed formal methods of selection. A majority of the instructors in the sample (8 out of 10) reported that they were appointed by 'personal contact.' The supervisors visited the villages and ascertained the willingness of people, who in their view, would satisfy the requirements to work as instructors. However, in two centres, where the supervisor found it difficult to appoint instructors the project officer and the supervisor together approached a few candidates and after getting their willingness appointed them as instructors.

As far as CROSS is concerned a different method of selection is adopted. This agency has established 'Village Sanghams' (associations) in a good number of villages in Bhongir Samithi which is its main area of operation. These 'Sanghams' were informed by the agecy about National Adult Education Programme and were asked to suggest the names of those interested for the post of instructors for undertaking teaching in the adult education centres. The candidates whose names were suggested by the Sanghams were selected by the agency and were appointed for two centres as instructors In the case of the third centre in the sample, as the village Sangham could not arrive at a consensus about any candidate the agency picked up a candidate who incidentally was also acceptable to the Sangham.

Thus the methods of selection adopted by all agencies in the sample differed though not drastically. By and large they have been guided by the exigencies of the situation. No doubt the investigator come across instances of nepotism and also role of subjective factors in the selection especially in the Sirsilla area where Andhra Mahila Sabha implemented the programme. As far as other agencies are concerned, the method of selection adopted by the Bhagavathula Charitable Trust has proved to be more rational compared to Durga Sangh Seva Samaj and Andhra Mahila Sabha. In the anxiety to entrust the job of teaching in the Adult Education Centre only to persons belonging to teaching profession the Durga Sangh Seva Samaj seems to have ignored other factors like age, interest, motivation, ability to teach and the capacity for running the Adult Education Centre. In the case of the Andhra Mahila Sabha also the investigator noticed such instances like selecting the instructors without taking into consideration their interest in the job. With this we shall now turn to the socio-economic background of instructors.

Socio-economic background of Instructors

In this section an attempt would be made to know the general background of the instructors. The standard variables that are usually employed to determine the socio-economic status like Age, Caste, Sex, Occupation, Education, Income are taken into consideration besides the teaching experience. The following table gives the age-wise distribution of the instructors.

TABLE 12

Age-wise distribution of Instructors

Sl. No	Category	Male	Female
1	15-25	8(50.00)	—
2	26-36	5(31.25)	3(100.00)
3	36-47	1(6.25)	—
4	48 & above	2(12.50)	—
Total		16(100.00)	3(100.00)

It is evident from the table that half of the male instructors in the sample fall in the age group of 15-25 years. Further about five male and three female instructors are aged between 26-36. The sample also consists of two instructors (12.50 per cent) who are above 48 years. It may be recalled that the Durga Sangh Seva Samaj has given preference to teachers in appointments to instructor posts. There were two retired teachers who are above 65 years.

Caste and Sex

Among nineteen instructors in the sample 16 are male instructors and three (15.78 per cent) are female instructors. Regarding caste background about 5 male instructors (31.25 per cent) and 1 female instructor (33.33 per cent) belong to scheduled caste, about 31.25 male instructors hail from backward classes. The representation of forward castes among instructors is about 37.50 per cent male and 66.27 per cent female.

Thus scheduled castes and backward castes constitute about 62.50 per cent among male instructors and 33.33 per cent among female instructors which is in conformity with the policy objectives. The female instructors are lesser in number in whole sample. With great difficulty the investigator could contact three instructors. The Government while admitting the agencies for grants stipulated that about fifty per cent of centres should be earmarked for women. None of the agencies in the sample could satisfy this requirement because of non-availability of women instructors and also learners.

TABLE 13

Caste and Sex-wise distribution of Instructors

Sl. No.	Name of the Caste	Male	Female
1	Scheduled Caste	5 (31.25)	5 (33.33)
2	Backward Caste	5 (31.25)	—
3	Forward Caste	6 (37.50)	2 (66.07)
	Total	16 (100.00)	3 (100.00)

Occupation

An analysis of the occupational background of the instructors is considered necessary in order to understand which occupational group is showing interest towards the adult education programme. The policy makers, as has already been pointed out, identified school teachers, students, village youth and ex-serviceman and retired personnel as the instructional cadre. The following table gives the occupational details of the instructors.

TABLE 14

Occupational background of Instructors

Sl. No.	Category	Male	Female
1	Agricultural Labour	1 (6.25)	—
2	Small Farmers	3 (18.75)	—
3	In-service Teachers	1 (6.25)	2 (66.27)
4	Educated Unemployed	9 (56.25)	—
5	Retired Teachers	2 (12.50)	—
6	Others	—	1 (33.33)

Of all the categories, educated unemployed constitute more than half of the instructors in the sample (56.25 per cent). About three instructors (18.75 per cent) of the sample belong to the small farmer category. There are three in-service teachers in the sample. Of them one is male instructor and two others are female instructors. Retired male teachers constitute about 12.50 per cent. It will be interesting to note that there is one agricultural labour who has been given opportunity to teach the adults by one of the agencies.

Thus an analysis of the occupational background reveals that majority of the instructors in the sample are educated unemployed followed by small farmers and retired teachers.

Income

The data on income of the instructors is gathered in order to ascertain which strata of income group is showing interest towards the programme. The following table gives details of the income of the instructors per month before they joined as instructors.

TABLE 15

Income-wise distribution of Instructors

Sl. No.	Slab	Male	Female
1	101-500	14 (87.50)	3 (100.00)
2	501-1000	2 (12.50)	—
3	1001-1500	—	—
4	1500 and above	—	—

As can be gleaned from the table, an overwhelming majority of instructors in the sample fall in the income range of Rs. 101-500 per month. While out of 16 male instructors 14 (87.50 per cent) earned between Rs. 101-500, all the female instructors belong to this range. Only two instructors have comfortable economic position as they belong to a higher category of income (501-1000). Thus the income level suggests that a majority of the instructors hail from very poor economic background.

Educational background

A study of the educational background of the instructors reveal that they possess sufficient educational background to teach in Adult Education Centres. The following table gives the agency-wise details of the educational qualifications of 19 respondents in the sample.

TABLE 16

Educational status of Instructors

Sl. No.	Agency	Qualifications						Total	
		S.S.C.		Inter		College			
		Male	Female	Male	Female	Male	Female	Male	Female
1.	A.M.S.	2	3	4	1	—	—	6	4
2.	B.C.T.	2	—	1	—	—	—	3	—
3.	CROSS	2	—	1	—	—	—	3	—
4.	D.S.S.	3	—	—	—	—	—	3	—

A majority of the instructors (63.15 per cent) in the sample possess secondary qualifications i.e. either tenth class or matriculation. The remaining instructors have done up to intermediate. Thus, the sample consists of fairly educated instructors which is considered as a good catchment area for implementation of Adult Education Programmes.

Previous experience

It is widely believed that it is relatively easy to shape a person with some experience and with some amount of educational background for adult education work rather than a notice. With this in view, the interview schedule convassed to the instructors carries a few questions relating to the previous experience in teaching, the details of which are presented below.

TABLE 17.

Previous experience in 'teaching'

Sl. No.	Type of experience	A.M.S. M	A.M.S. F	B.C.T. M	B.C.T. F	CROSS M	CROSS F	D.S.S. M	D.S.S. F	Total %
1	Taught adults	2	—	1	—	1	—	1	—	5 (26.33)
2	Private teaching	1	—	1	—	2	—	—	—	4 (21.11)
3	Taught children in school	—	—	—	—	—	—	2	—	2 (10.35)
4	No experience	3	4	1	—	—	—	—	—	8 (42.21)
	Total	6	4	3	--	3	—	3	—	19 (100.00)

The table is self explanatory. Of the nineteen instructors in the sample about 26.33 per cent had some experience in teaching adults while 21.11 per cent of instructors have reported that they have 'some' teaching experience before joining as instructors. About 10.53% were full fledged teachers in upper primary schools. It may be mentioned here that the policy outline on National Adult Education Programme indicated the inevitability of relying on teachers for taking up the instructors positions, though purely on voluntary basis and through method of selection.[7]

Reasons for taking up Instructors' job

The instructors were asked to state the reasons for accepting the appointment as instructor. Eight out of ten instructors appointed by Andhra Mahila Sabha stated that they took up the job to supplement their income. Two instructors have cited that they were very much interested in teaching adults. The instructors appointed by B C T stated that they took up the job because it afforded some financial assistance, but also because it gave them an opportunity to take part in the developmental activities of B C T. They felt that besides providing some financial relief, the agency also gave them a chance to participate in its activities. It may be recalled here that the B C T has been a well reputed organizations and a majority of the people in Yellamanchili area knew various activities of the agency. Similarly all the three instructors in the Bhongir area which is the main operational area of CROSS stated that they were interested in taking any activity sponsored by the agency. Incidentally this organization places high premium on education of masses as a liberator from exploitation. The researcher noticed commendable identity of the instructors in the sample with the main objectives of the agency. Coming to the instructors of Durga Sangh Seva Samaj which has implemented the programme in Gannavaram block, out of three instructors in the sample two stated that they took up the job only to supplement their income. The other respondent cited his keen interest in the programme.

Thus nearly half of the respondents stated their interest in the programme the remaining half cited economic and other reasons.

Training Programme

Training occupies an important place in the adult education programme as the National Adult Education Programme is stated as qualitatively and quantitatively superior to earlier Adult Education Programmes. The training of instructors is considered critical for the success of the programme as he/she is the key level or front-line worker.[8] Further, the policy makers of the programme viewed training programme as an exercise in self knowledge or value clarification to the trainees.[9] Besides, it has been observed in one of the documents released by the Directorate of Adult Education that the training programme "is fundamentally a process of . . . education and has to reflect the main characteristics of the methodology that the functionaries would have to follow while working with the learning groups at the block level".[10]

All the instructors reported that they had undergone training after induction, although differences as to the length or duration and training among the agencies is noticed. While the B C T arranged a training programme for 27 days, the Andhra Mahila Sabha, the Comprehensive Rural Operations Service Society, and the Durga Sangh Seva Samaj arranged training programmes for 15, 14, 15 days respectively. All the agencies in the sample trained their instructional cadre in two phases. The venue for the training programme is their head quarters in case of two organizations the B C T at Yellamanchili and the CROSS at Bhongir while Mahila Sabha and Durga Sangh Seva Samaj conducted training programmes closer to their areas of operation.

The content of the training programme for instructors did not vary much from among the sample agencies. All the agencies in the sample arranged lectures by experts from outside. However, B C T and CROSS have taken special care to make the training programmes 'discussion oriented' rather than lecture oriented. The participants were encouraged to simulate the situations usually faced by illiterate adults in rural areas. The project officer and others clarified doubts raised by the instructors.[11] The instructors in these two agencies (BCT & CROSS) seem to have been extremely satisfied that is the case with other instructors of other agencies in the sample. The respondents in the sample were asked by the investigator to comment on the utility of the training programmes. About 9 out of 10 instructors in the centres run by Andhra Mahila Sabha and Durga Sangh Seva Samaj rated their programme as 'not adequate' while all the instructors of BCT and CROSS rated them as 'extremely useful'.

While the instructors of centres under A.M.S. and D.S.S. rated their training as 'inadequate' others confined its utility. Training as a critical input to achieve the policy objective appears to have been very well articulated by the organizers of the programme in B C T and CROSS.

Perceptions about objectives of N A E P

In order to gauge the difference between NAEP and the earlier programmes to educate illiterate adults, the investigator asked a few questions about the objectives of NAEP. All the instructors of Andhra Mahila Sabha in the sample stated that literacy as the main objective. Only four out of ten could tell the other component the functional education and much less could tell (only two) the third component of the programme i.e. the awareness. In contrast, the instructors under B.C.T., CROSS, and D.S.S. listed out all the components of the programme. One major difference between the earlier programmes to educate illiterates and NAEP is that while the earlier one's focussed mainly on literacy (or 3 R's) the NAEP widened it and includes functionality and social awareness also besides literacy. Absence of appreciation of the other two points out to the inadequate training programmes of some agencies.

Weightage

Regarding weightage to each of the three components stated above 7 out of 10 instructors under Andhra Mahila Sabha told that more weightage was given to literacy component and three reported that along with literacy functional education also was given coverage only a couple of instructors at least felt the need to give equal weightage to all the components of the programme.

Coming to B.C.T. although preference seems to have been given to literacy the other two components are not totally neglected. Since B.C.T. has been engaged in some productive programmes, which are found to be useful to the people in general in that area, it has succeeded to certain extent to motivate learners to attend Adult Education Centres. The agency has announced through its instructors that preference in admission to carpentry training centres run by it would be given to those who continuously attend Adult Education Centres for ten months. Moreover, the Project Officer, Supervisors and others have taken interest in arranging lectures pertaining to social awareness. The learners were also taught some rudimentary techniques in carpentry, pottery and other such trades.

As far as CROSS is concerned we notice relatively more emphasis on literacy and next to literacy, the awareness component seems to have been given preference. The instructors reported difficulties in implementing functional education component mainly owing to lack of study material as well as infrastructure.

The instruction by Durga Sangh Seva Samaj also gave importance to literacy component as attested by instructors. Two out of three instructors brought to the notice of the investigator the limitations in the implementation of functional education and social awareness components. Only one instructor stated that in his instruction all the three components were covered with only marginal success.[12]

Thus the perceptions of the respondents on the objectives of NAEP are not very satisfactory. By and large the agencies have given preference to literacy component alone. Further, excepting B.C.T. and CROSS other agencies did not seem to have accorded priority to other components of the programme. This points to the inadequacies in publicity to the NAEP in general and non-appreciation of the value of functional education and social awareness to the cause of adult education. If policy components are not fully comprehended, there may arise a problem when they are being implemented.

Instructors' reaction to the Method of identification of learners

A majority of the instructors (14 out of 19) adopted the method of identification of learners enrolled in adult education centres through personal contact. Some instructors reported that they orally enquired about the age, caste, interest and former educational background of adult illiterates in their villages. All the instructors belonging to B.C.T. were asked to conduct a survey of the entire village. CROSS, however, entrusted the task of selecting learners to its village sanghams with the help of instructors. All the ten instructors in the sample belonging to Andhra Mahila Sabha (AMS) relied on the personal identification method. In the case of the Gannavaram block where the Durga Sangh Seva Samaj (DSS) conducted the programme, two instructors told the researcher that they 'knew' all the adults who were illiterates and felt no necessity for a survey. However, one instructor in the sample told that he selected learners after enquiring about their background.

It appears that the 'survey' for identification of learners in AMS, DSS is not foolproof and reflects the agencies' casual way of treating the most important aspect of the programme.

Instructors' reaction to the Method of motivating learners

Here it must be pointed out that apart from their regular tasks of giving instruction in the curriculum, the agencies included some supplementary devices aimed at motivating the learners to go through and benefit from the programme. In this, the instructors are again to play a vital role. It is about this supplementary tasks towards motivation that we now deal with.

There are broadly two methods adopted by the agencies : (1) personal contact between learners and the instructors, (2) arranging frequent contacts between the officials of the agency and the learners. The instructors of AMS and DSS as has already been stated relied heavily on personal contacts in which the instructor was told continuously to highlight the benefits of adult education. Eight out of nineteen instructors reported using various methods like persuasion to attract and retain learners, while six instructors of the BCT and CROSS highlighted the role of their respective agencies in the development of the locality, and the people that is by projecting their agencies role as 'change agents'. By this method, they succeeded, to some extent, in controlling the dropout problem. This has been corroborated by learners also. Some of the instructors under BCT, CROSS reported that those who attended adult education centres for 10 months will be offered loans and various other inputs.[13] Instructors of other agencies in the sample have not shown keen interest in motivating the learners except by occasional lectures.[14] Thus we notice prevalence and different methods of motivating.

The investigator sought suggestions for motivating learners. An interesting aspect to be noted here is that the instructors belonging to BCT and CROSS recommended for a preferential treatment to the learners in the distribution of loans and other benefits which these organisations arrange for, besides equalizing the 10 month course with 5th class in the formal system so as to enable the learners to get into such jobs like watchman, gateman etc.[15] The instructors of other agencies suggested economic incentives to the learners. These suggestions reveal that there is not one single method of motivating adults either to attend or to continue in the programme. The trend confirms the popular view that incentives of some kind motivate villagers to take interest in any developmental programme.

Teaching/learning materials

The views of the instructional cadre on the material used are elicited with a view to improving them. All the instructors in the same reported the receipt of teaching material. However, they differed on the relevance of study/teaching material. A large number of instructors of the centres under Andhra Mahila Sabha reported that the material supplied to them deals mainly with aspects relating to agriculture. The same appears to be the case with the teaching/learning material supplied by CROSS, which has incidentally prescribed the material produced by AMS. The BCT prescribed and supplied books prepared exclusively for N A E P by Adult Education Department of the Andhra University. Although the instructors were not unhappy about the contents, out of three responding to the queries, two complained about the small size of the print of the material. On examination of the material supplied to the learners by the Andhra Mahila Sabha, it was found that the books were prepared keeping in view a specific project i.e. Farmers Functional Literacy (FFL). Needless to say, that the objective of FFL Programme and N A E P are different.[16] Some of the instructors as well as supervisors who earlier worked in F F L programme corroborated this fact. When the investigator enquired about the material, the authorities concerned had not given a convincing answer. This would prove how organizations tend to perceive the policy objectives. Though one may argue that the material is not totally irrelevant, one gets an impression that the attitude of AMS is one of easy taking of the new policy to educate illiterate adults.

Support and Co-operation received

One of the ideas of policy planners of NAEP is to make the programme as broad based as possible thereby putting an end to the tendency of treating adult education as the concern of education departments alone. The investigator attempted to ascertain the co-operation received from other departments especially the local leaders and other developmental functionaries of the government. Though the instructors reported good co-operation from their superiors within the organization, almost all were sore about the indifferent attitude of the government officials toward the programme (16 out of 19). A good majority of instructors rated as poor the co-operation given by local leaders (14 out of 19). They felt that their supervisors helped them in many ways in organizing and location of centres, in enlisting the support of local political functionaries as well as in keeping up the morale of the instructors. A few instructors (5/19) also reported the authoritarian attitude of the supervisors as well as project officers. It is interesting to note here that the instructors who were selected on the recommendations of their local leaders, received some support in running adult education centres.[17] Some instructors faced a tough problem in locating an adult centre owing to the stiff opposition of local leaders. A few instructors narrated how the elite disliked the very idea of educating adults. Some brushed aside the idea of adult education, while others warned the consequences of imparting education to the illiterates in their areas. Their main fear as reported by the instructors was, that, if the masses are educated, it will not be possible for the vested interests to deal with them in the way they do when they are illiterates, uneducated and ignorant. That is why, according to some instructors the local leaders opposed establishment of centres in their villages. When the instructor refused to listen, he was harassed in many ways asking him to pay back all his dues, transferring him to a remote place, suggesting that the loan amount be paid from adult education funds, or from learners. Further, the learners were advised not to attend and when they flouted the writ they were asked to immediately repay their loans. In such hostile environment, the instructor, howsoever effective he is, fails to find a solution and prefers to close down the centre for sometime. Some learners held him responsible for bringing in a new set of problems for their already problem ridden life. Such situation further demoralised the instructor. As for the co-operation of government officials, as stated earlier only three out of the nineteen respondents stated that the officials were extending the necessary co-operation. However, there are some saving features. For example, in the centres visited by the governmental functionaries the instructors reported good reception to the lectures by them. Thus, a majority of instructors feel that more co-operation is needed from local leaders and government officials in running adult education centres effectively.

Instructors : Their problems

All the instructors are expected to approach their supervisor first and then the project officer in case they experience any difficulty in running adult education centres. This supports the view that, even in non-governmental agencies, the practice of respecting hierarchical norms and bureaucratisation is present.

The type of problems which occasioned the instructors seeking the guidance of their immediate supervisors related to matters like fall in the attendance of the learners and how to retrieve the situation. Non-cooperation of village elite/leaders in running adult education centres and also deliberate attempts to close down the centres in some instances, delays, and difficulties in the receipt of learning material and in matters relating to the availability of other material facilities like lighting and problems with the behaviour of learners in the class rooms instances of learners coming under the influence of drink and teasing of women participants in co-education classes did arise occasionally.

The response of the supervisors on the whole is reported to be encouraging. In many cases complaints about material necessities were personally solved by the supervisors themselves intervening either with the government officials or with the local elite. This was particularly visible in the case of supervisors belonging to BCT and CROSS. The role of supervisors belonging to Durga Sangh Seva Samaj and AMS seems less encouraging. Where the village elite/leaders attempted to close down the centres the supervisors and project officers visited them and attempted to persuade them. In some places it worked and in some others it led to further trouble.

Thus co-ordination between the instructor and his immediate supervisors appears satisfactory. Further, there is evidence that good rapport existed between the instructors and the supervisiors generial. It is more or less a uniform opinion of the instructors in the sample that supervisors were sincere in exhorting the instructors to operate the programme in the proper spirit by constant reminding of the ideals of the programme. A general spirit of confidence was thus instilled in the instructor thanks to the positive interaction between the instructors and supervisors.

On the issue of the desirability of transfer of instructors from one centre to another for every three months nearly half of the respondents (8/19) did not agree with this, only one fourth (5/19) favoured it, others remained non-committal. One respondent, however, pointed out the practical difficulties of in service' teachers who cannot move around. The practice however, has been that the instructors were allotted to particular centres and no transfers were made. While the opinion of the instructors on transfers was largely negative, some instructors, however, agreed to the suggestion of the researcher that a periodical change of instructors would be better as it would expose them to different types of people. There is thus a clear difference in the views of the instructors on this issue. The learners too were divided on this issue. Whatever be the merits of 'transfer', it would appear that, given the fact that some instructors are only part-time with a separate full-time job, transfers would prove to be extremely inconvenient to them. Apart from this practical difficulty, as the recommendation is that instructors should be drawn from the locality and community in which the centre is located, policy wise too transfers are perhaps undesirable.

Opinion on learners' achievements

An overwhelming majority of the instructors (18/19) felt that at least 50 per cent of the learners acquired the skills of reading and writing and some amount of knowledge in arithmetic. An inter-agency comparison reveal that the instructors of BCT and CROSS are quite positive about the impact of literacy component on the learners. The instructors of DSS and AMS, however, felt that only 40-45 per cent of the learners enrolled in their respective adult education centres could improve their reading, writing and numerical abilities.

Almost all learners (17/19) pointed out the difficulties involved in imparting skills in functional education and in raising the awareness. The main reasons for their failure is lack of infrasctrutural facilities and proper learning materials. Some instructors regretted that instruction was confined to face-to-face teaching, Except black board no other teaching aid is made available. Perhaps audio-visual aids like radio, tape recorder and TV would go a long way in sustaining the interest of and VCR the learners. Thus the instructors were modest about their claims as far as achievement in the three components of the programme are concerned.

Job Satisfaction

Views on job satisfaction as expressed by instructors show wide variance. A good majority of the respondents (12/19) reported that they were satisfied with their jobs. The remaining (5/19) were totally dissatisfied with their jobs for a host of reasons which include meagre remuneration, heavy work, apathy and politics played by the local leaders[18] and indifference of the government officials and authoritarian attitude of the supervisors and project officers. Two respondents have refused to react on this question.

Suggestions for increasing the effectiveness of the Programme

The suggestions given by the instructors touch several aspects of the programme administration. An overwhelming majority (87.8 per cent) wanted increase in tne honorarium.[19] Most of them said that an honorarium of Rs. 50/- per month was very meagre (it was enhanced to Rs. 100/- recently) and the requirements of the job demand lot of their attention and time. About 48.9 per cent suggested that unless some economic incentives were offered to the learners it would be difficult to sustain the interest of an illiterate adult. A good percentage of instructors (46.9) also suggested the need for more diversified teaching and learning materials. Some suggested association of village level politicians with all aspects of programme management. The other suggestions include strong linkages with other development programmes (22.88), proper lighting facilities (52.33), increasing the involvement of government functionaries (70.3), co-operation of village elite (57.33). Suggestions like less paper work, conducting regular tests, motivating the learners who show encouraging improvement by offering economic incentives are grouped under "other" suggestions which constitute about 43.81 per cent.

The instructors' reactions in the sample on various aspects of the programme thus suggest that there are clear gaps in the training programme, conducted by some agencies. However, it should be remembered that they were not totally disoriented towards the programme. It was given to understand that lectures as part of the training programme arranged by Andhra Mahila Sabha and Durga Sangh Seva Samaj are mostly stereotyped. And this had produced a negative effect on the trainees. As has aptly been commented by one of the trainees, "It appears silly if a resource person tells me how to look after my agricultural farm or how and when the paddy should be cut as a good number in the group hail from agricultural background".[20] The agencies which organized training programmes have not even used audio-visual aids to sustain the interest of instructors. A couple of instructors were frustrated at the general attitude of the village elites. They felt that good programmes like adult education fail because of polluted political atmosphere. Thus the training programmes appear to be not strongenough especially with regard to a couple of agencies in the sample. The Durga Sangh Seva Samaj in particular does not seem to be knowing that the NAEP is not a literacy programme alone but also contains two other components, functionality and awareness. The agency does not also seem to be aware of the fact that mere literacy drives will not succeed.

Coming specifically to the problem of co-ordination, we notice that purely in terms of the instructors on the one hand and the supervisors on the other, there has been adequate co-ordination. But co-ordination does not merely pertain to rapport and personal relationships. A greater effort on the part of the agencies to equip the centres would not only improve the programme but will contribute to increased morale in the instructors. In other words, a more intensive and constant interaction between the agency and the centre would generate a correspondingly greater degree of involvement as far as the instructors and other cadres are concerned.

Views of Supervisory staff

In the organizational framework of NAEP, the tasks of supervisors would be concerned with making instructors effective in the field.[21] The supervisors are expected to guide and spport the work of a cluster of about 30 adult education centres as visualized in the administrative structure of a project.[22] The main functions of the supervisor as conceived by the policy makers of NAEP include (1) to enlist community co-operation and support, (2) to help in the survey of the area and assess the learners' needs, (3) to help in the training programmes of instructors, (4) to help prepare flexible and need based curricula and materials, (5) to plan and organize the programme, (6) to keep open the channels of communication, (7) to evaluate and guide the work of the centres and (8) to take steps to give wide publicity to the programme.[23]

The supervisors are expected to perform the above functions with the support and co-operation of project officer, development departments of the government, the instructors, resource persons from among the local people and above all with the help of the community.

In this section an attempt is made first to analyse the socio-economic status of the supervisors, their perception about the objectives of NAEP, their selection, recruitment and training methods of supervision, comments on resource material, steps initiated to secure co-ordination internally as well as externally, mechanisms to monitor the programme, job satisfaction and finally their impressions and suggestions.

Socio-economic status

In this such standard variables like age, caste, and sex, education, economic, occupational status of the four supervisors in the sample will be briefly analysed in order to determine their socio-economic profile.

Age : Of the four supervisors two belong to the age group of 25-34 years and the other two fall between 35-44 age group. The supervisory staff of all the agencies therefore satisfied the requirement prescribed by the policy planners that the supervisors should at least be of 21 years.[24]

Sex and Caste : All the supervisors in the sample are male. Among them three are from forward castes and one belongs to backward caste.

Educational status : All the supervisors are fairly educated. Three out of 4 are graduates while the fourth one has studied up to twelfth class (or plus two equivalent). The supervisory cadre of the sample possess more than prescribed qualifications for the post which is in consonance with the policy objectives of AEP.[25]

Occupation : Occupation wise, two supervisors are teachers and one a homeopathic doctor and the other an employee of the agency. Among the two teachers one is working as a full time employee of the agency on deputation from Zilla Parishad School. The other one is just attending to work on part-time basis.

Income : All the supervisors belong to middle income group.

Previous experience : On the experience in adult education work, two out of four have previous experience in adult education and the other two are new to the job.

Thus the socio-economic background of the supervisors

reveals that all of them are in the prescribed age group, and a majority are graduates. All of them belong to middle income group.

Opinions on objectives

All the supervisors are aware of the three main objectives i.e. literacy, functional education and social awareness. However, they are divided in their opinion about the weightage to be given to each of the three components. The supervisor belonging to B C T drew the attention of the investigator to the impracticability of implementing functionality component as it involves large scale preparation. The supervisor of CROSS on the other hand is of the opinion that awareness is more important than functionality. Coming to the D S S though the supervisor is aware of the three components, he appears to be more interested in imparting three R's rather than the other two components. The case with the A M S is altogether different. The supervisor of this agency said that for imparting any thing, literacy is most important. In his opinion the material supplied by his agency to the learners is out of tune with the objectives of N A E P and hence questions on weightage does not arise at all.

Selection, Recruitment and Training

The criteria for selection and recruitment of supervisors as conceived by policy planners of the N A E P is as follows :

(1) As far as possible, the supervisors should be drawn from among the ranks of experienced and successful adult education teachers, extension workers, N S V S, N S S and Community Social Service Volunteers, social workers and also those who may have academic qualification in adult education.

(2) They should be familiar with the local language, and as far as possible be residents of the project or a similar area. They must be willing to live in the cluster area to which they are eventually allotted.[26]

We also find reference to modern methods of recruitment in various policy documents. One of such method is to ask the interested candidates for the post of spervisors to submit in advance a full and honest account of their understanding of the N A E P, the tasks of the supervisor within this and the assessment of their suitability for the post.

Coming to the response from the supervisors about their selection, one supervisor (belonging to B C T) replied that he was just asked to look after the programme through an official memorandum. Further he said, he happens to be one of the co-ordinators of the agency put in charge of rural leadership programmes. The agency might have thought that he can look after the adult education programme as well. As has already been pointed out in the last section of the first chapter on profiles of the agencies, the Bhagavathula Charitable Trust is engaged in implementing a variety of programmes/projects in Yellamanchili block. That way this agency is placed in a better position vis-a-vis others in the sample. As part of the developmental programmes the agency sponsored and ran a few non-formal adult education centres too. The supervisor of N A E P of this agency looked after those centres and the same person was made Project Officer-cum-Supervisor of the N A E P of this agency. Hence no formal method of selection of supervisor was felt necessary by the agency.

The Durga Sangh Seva Samaj too did not follow any formal methods in the selection of supervisors. In fact the Honorary Project Officer in charge of the A E P appointed his own son as the supervisor. It is also noteworthy that the project officer himself is none other than Director of the agency. This instance brings to light the special problems or considerations that arise when a voluntary social service agency undertakes the adult education work as one of the items of its activities. In some cases the head of the agency can himself become the head of the adult education programme. This has the advantage of solving the problems of co-ordination as the head of the agency himself is incharge of the A E P. On the other hand, this may mean that the programme may not receive the requisite attention given the project officer's busy engagements with other activities.

The supervisor of N A E P for this agency is full time teacher in a school in Vijayawada which is about 20 KMs from the area of operation. In spite of his best efforts he could not strike a balance between his official responsibilities as a teacher in a school, and as supervisor of an adult education project. Some adult education centres are located as far away as 35 to 40 KMs. Distance naturally deterred the supervisor from undertaking frequent visits to adult education centres which are so necessary for ensuring their effective functioning. The Project Officer is quite an aged man and visits by him are totally ruled out. With the result, there is noticeable laxity in supervision. These things point out how voluntary agencies exhibit tendencies which may have negative effect on the objectives of a qualitative programme like adult education. It is not to say ll the agencies suffer from such an inadequacy.

The Comprehensive Rural Operations Service Society appointed the co-ordinator of its adult education programmes as the supervisor. The agency did not follow formal methods for selection of its supervisor taking into consideration the experience of the candidate.

With regard to Andhra Mahila Sabha, it has advertised the posts of supervisors and selected three candidates out of fifteen applied. The selection committee consisted of the Chairman and Secretary of the Literacy House (which looks after education programmes as the name itself indicates) and the Project Officer. However, it was given to understand that no expert in adult education seems to have been associated with the selection committee.

Thus the method of selection of supervisors through advertisement was followed by only one agency. The other agencies in the sample selected and appointed the supervisors without official formalities. The reason could be that these agencies had more confidence in the personnel readily available in their organisations.

Training

The training programmes to supervisors are intended to increase the understanding about the N A E P and the needs of the community and learners, impart the ability to prepare material work out, methods of organizing adult education centres, evolve techniques for gaining community support, increase their ability for planning the follow up programmes, develop skills arranging training programme for instructors and finally enhance competence on various ways of achieving the co-ordination with other developmental programmes/departments.[27] Besides these, the policy makers of N A E P recommended provision for practical experience in order to acquire skills necessary to perform their functions with confidence.

The organisers of the training programmes for supervisors are expected to arrange :

(1) Visits to villages for getting an acquaintance with the needs of learners and learning environment;
(2) Development of suitable programmes based on the field data collected through surveys;
(3) Preparation of need-based curriculum or adaptations of existing, available curriculum;
(4) Evaluation of the available teaching/learning material;
(5) Acquaintance with the procedures of monitoring (monthly, quarterly and annual reports);
(6) Preparation and use of simple visual aids.

The above are some of the functions that are supposed to be experimented by the supervisors in the course of the training programme.[28]

The Central Directorate of Adult Education suggested that there be a two or three phased training programme, for supervisors starting with a three day initial orientation programme followed by two week pre-service training and further followed by a "process of recurrent training sessions through monthly meetings, refresher courses and correspondences".[29]

Thus training for the supervisors was visualised as a process of continuous learning.

Now, coming to the training part of the supervisors in the sample, it was found that all the supervisors did undergo training at the Sri Venkateswara University, Tirupati. The State Directorate of Adult Education, Government of Andhra Pradesh sponsored the training programme. The State Resources Centre, Tirupati conducted the programme. The duration of the programme is spread over a period of 10 days.

The supervisors of B.C.T. and D.S.S. attend the training a few weeks before the inauguration of the adult education programme in their area. The supervisors of CROSS and AMS, however, could attend the programme after the starting of the adult-centres in their areas.

All the supervisors opined that the training programme attended by them was mainly lecture oriented. They were not given an opportunity by the organisers of the training programme to narrate individually or collectively to share their experiences for the benefit of the fellow supervisors in adult education work. In fact, a supervisor called the whole training a 'farce'. Coming to the utility of the lectures delivered in the training course, out of four supervisors, three felt that these were 'idealistic', miles away from realities in rural areas. Two supervisors felt that they did not understand some lectures owing to language problems. The regional language being Telugu, it is no wonder that the supervisors experienced some difficulty in following lectures in English. The investigator was further told that the supervisors in the training programmes were not encouraged to participate, be it in the form of discussions or other simulation exercises. The whole programme was a one-sided affair. A supervisor summed up the programme saying that the organisers of the training programme should first attend programme on how to organise training programmes to the key level functionaries of the N.A.E.P. Questioning the methods of training, yet another supervisor felt that the grasp of the organisers of training programme about rural areas in general and about the psychology of rural people in particular is so poor that he felt like withdrawing himself from the training programme half way through.

Regarding the material that they are supposed to receive, all the four supervisors said that they did not receive any. When a supervisor asked the organisers about the material, it seems he was told that he would get them by post. He waited for three months and got reconciled to the indifference of the organisers. On the utility of the lectures, two supervisors said that whatever little they could understand sounded 'upstartish', to them. A particular mention need to be made about "how to organise training programmes to the instructors". Two lectures it seems were given on the above theme. The supervisors were told that they should involve other developmental functionaries in the programme. A respondent in the sample remarked that the indifference of the developmental functionaries was experienced by the organisers of the training programme as out of five lectures arranged to such *developmental personnel only two turned up. And, their performance* was also poor. Thus the supervisor told the investigator that "it is very easy to preach than to practice". Enquired about the field visits they were supposed to undertake during the training programme, all the supervisors in the sample said that they were not taken any where.

The above instances show the gap between the directives of the policy planner and the implementors. What is the main reason for the discontentment of the supervisors about their training ? The trainees say that it was because of the half-hearted efforts of the organisers. It surprised the investigator as to how the personnel of S R C could bc so indifferent even to the medium of lectures. The fact that a good number reported their difficulties in following the lectures in English on the first day of the training programme itself and the consequent failure of the organisers to remedy the situation, clearly exhibit the formalistic/ritualistic response of the organisers of training programmes. Further the failure to encourage participation in debates and discussions reveals the unchanged nature of the organisers towards training programmes. As aptly summed up by a participant, "the commitment of N A E P which they often exhorted us to cultivate, appears to be lacking in them".

Methods of Supervision

The effective supervisory methods seen to have been by almost all respondents in the sample. These include (a) regular visits (scheduled and surprise) to the A E C under their control ; (b) checking the attendance, (c) guiding the instructors on methods of teaching, (d) getting the feedback on regularity of instructor ; (e) method of teaching and (f) enquiring about the difficulties faced by learners.

Inter-agency comparison, however, proved that the two supervisors of B C T and CROSS are far more effective vis-a-vis their counterparts in Durga Sangh Seva Samaj and Andhra Mahila Sabha. In terms of number of visits to A E Cs the investigator noticed that the supervisors of the B C T and CROSS checked more number of centres in a day than the other two supervisors in the sample, which is of course made possible mainly due to the fact that the supervisors of BCT and CROSS are provided with vehicles. Because of this, on an average they could visit six centres per day. The supervisors of A M S and D S S could visit only one or two centres per day as they have to commute the long distances by other modes of transport. That is why instructors of the B C T and CROSS reported a more number of surprise inspections by their supervisors. In case of instructors of A M S and D S S this was not the case and they could not take up as many 'surprise' visits as was the case with the supervisors of B C T and CROSS. Moreover, as the two agencies (BCT & CROSS) are involved in a number of economic programmes and a readily available infrastructure running Adult Education programme posed no fresh infrastructural and other problem. Each agency as a matter of fact has got two to three motor vehicles besides jeeps etc. That is why they could be able to maintain an effective supervision. So it must be understood that factors like conveyance also play an important role in ensuring effective supervision.

Arranging lectures by resource persons

We have mentioned earlier how the policy planners visualised A E P as the concern of the departments and should not be viewed as the job of educationists alone. Involvement of others like the Block Development Officer (BDO), managers of banks, project officials and small farmers development agency and other officials in-charge of agriculture, animal husbandry etc., is regarded as crucial for the success. The supervisors were asked about the role of other developmental functionaries. A number of reasons were cited by the supervisors for their inadequate role. The first is the indifference. Only one supervisor belonging to B C T could succeed to some extent, in persuading the officials in the block to visit some of the centres. But it was mainly because of the image of the agency in that part of the state. Right since its inception, it made sincere serious efforts to associate the block level officials in almost all its activities. The rapport it has established over a period of time was utilised by the supervisor atleast to some extent which resulted in getting some co-operation from them.

But coming to the other two agencies, Durga Sanga Seva Samaj and Andhra Mahila Sabha, they do not have strong roots in the areas where they have implemented the programme. And naturally they had to encounter difficulty right from starting the project. These two agencies could not involve the block level functionaries in the programme to the extent they desired partly owing to 'unacquaintance' with the area and also partly due to indifference of the local level village elite. Further the investigator came to know that the agencies did not seek co-operation from either local leaders or officials.

With regard to CROSS it could not involve block level developmental functionaries for a very significant reason. The very fact that CROSS's long standing work in the area seemed to have led to strained relations between block level officials and CROSS. This is because CROSS in pursuing the other aspects of its activities and as a matter of fact had on many occasions crossed swords with the block administration. For example, on issues like fertilizer distribution CROSS did not fight shy of taking up matters with the block officials wherever malpractices in distribution of fertilizers were identified. In any case, the block officials got the impression that there were instances of CROSS instigating some rural sections to vocally complain against block officials. This is an interesting instance of close contacts between a voluntary agency and a rural government resulting in estrangement rather than co-operation. To an extent, this should be assumed as a given factor. In such circumstances problems of co-ordination in the implementation of a policy like Adult Education, arising out of the lack of rapport between the agency and the government becomes inevitable. The agency organized several processions against rise in prices of essential commodities, for establishment of fair-price shops in villages, for distribution of fertilisers with subsidy to the needy etc. It brought to the notice of higher officials in the district about the rampant corruption at village and mandal levels and demanded stern action against corrupt administrators. Thus CROSS has established itself as an agency of masses and earned the name of crusader for justice to the unorganised rural people. The activities of the agency to an extent antagonized the local bureaucracy. The landlords joined with police and taluq officials made several efforts to close down the agency by using all sorts of pressures and attacks but they could not succeed. This only shows how dedicated voluntary agencies are harassed with a view to continuing the status quo.

Thus the methods of supervision adopted by the supervisors in the sample seem to be satisfactory. The checking of attendance registers and paying surprise visits did to an extent keep the instructors on alert. However, coming to the checking of the drop out rate is concerned, where the instructors failed, the supervisor also did not succeed much. Except the supervisors of the BCT and CROSS who tried and succeeded to some extent in helping the learners in their problems like securing a loan, settling disputes between two castes etc., the other supervisors in the sample could not do anything as they neither have access to other institutions which could do something to the learners nor could act in co-operation with officials concerned at the block/taluq level in finding a solution to some of the problems faced by the learners.

On the whole, one comes to the conclusion that the supervisory methods are satisfactory but there is a limit to what they can do as the problems of increasing the effectiveness of supervisors would depend on various other factors which are mostly beyond the control of the supervisor.

Resource Material

All the supervisors reported that they distributed teaching/learning material for instruction to the instructors. Regarding the source of the material, the Andhra Mahila Sabha produced and supplied to the learner the material prepared by it. The

Department of Adult Education, Andhra University prepared primers for learners in the centres run by it under N A E P—University Adult Education Programme. The same material was ordered and used for its learners in Centres under the Bhagavathula Charitable Trust. The Comprehensive Rural Operations Service Society supplied to its learners the material prepared by Andhra Mahila Sabha. The Durga Sangh Seva Samaj acquired the material prepared by a private publisher. An attempt is also made to elicit the views of the supervisory personnel on utility and the relevance of the material in general. Of the four supervisors in sample, two supervisors felt that the material supplied is not totally irrelevant and felt that much needed to be done to revise or refashion the material in the light of the feedback from the learners. The other two supervisors opined that the material supplied meets the occasion.

All the supervisors reported the receipt of the material in adequate number. However, as has already been observed, the A M S in this respect is in a better position compared to others in the sample. The material which was prepared by it for another programme (Farmers Functional Literacy Programme) was reprinted at its own press in Hyderabad and it did not face any problem in its supply. It distributed a set consisting of six books to each learner. But the B C T and D S S distributed one book to each of the learners and CROSS distributed two books. The supervisors were by and large satisfied with the distribution part.

Co-ordination : Mechanism and Process

As has already been discussed, the success of programmes like N A E P depends to a large extent on how best the co-ordination is achieved or secured. The investigator examined the operation of the principle of co-ordination in the implementation of N A E P through voluntary agencies in the sample.

In this section an examination of the mechanism created by each agency for achieving co-ordination is attempted. Broadly, there appears to be two bodies for securing co-ordination. One at the agency level for the purpose of the study called 'project level committee' and the other at the village level or adult education centre level, called 'village level committee'. It must be remembered that not all agencies have a two-tier co-oridinating bodies. Again these bodies are referred to with different names.[30]

Of the two bodies intended to secure coordination discussion is more on project level committee, as the village level committees of almost all the agencies in the sample remained dysfunctional. The discussion that follows begins with the structure and functions of the Project Level Committees (P L C's).

The Project Level Committee (P L C)

It must be mentioned that the functions of the P L Cs are not precisely and exhaustively given in any documents relating to any of the agencies. It is possible to identify them both from what is contained in some other documents[31] and from an informal study of their functioning.

The main functions of the P L Cs include (i) to secure Co-ordination between adult education programme and other programmes by the other development agencies ; (ii) to ensure co-ordination between adult education programmes and other formal systems of education ; (iii) to create necessary administrative infrastructure and supervision ; (iv) to arrange lectures by resource persons and identifying the persons belonging to the developmental departments of the government for the same ; (v) to make arrangements for the supply of reading material to the learners ; (vi) to fix criteria for selection of supervisors, instructors and arranging for their training ; (vii) to lay broad guidelines for managing day-to-day administration ; (viii) to continuously monitor the progress by adhering to the proformae ; and (ix) to take steps to associate local elite in the programme.

Membership

The membership of the P L Cs varied from one agency to the other. The Chairman of this body in BCT and CROSS was the Secretary and the head of the agency respectively. The Chairmanship of the P L C of D S S was kept vacant. The

Project Officer is made as the Convenor of the body. However, the A M S nominated the President of the Panchayat Samithi of the Sirsilla Block as the Chairman of its P L C. Regarding membership, the B C T had involved the supervisor and one third of its total number of instructors. For every three months the representation of instructors changed and almost all instructors took part in the deliberations of the body at one time or the other. Local leaders and learners are also associated sometimes with the P L C meetings.

The Project Level Committee of the CROSS comprised the Chairman, Supervisor and three instructors besides other functionaries. It is given to understand that the learners are also invited sometimes to the meetings. But the criteria of learners/instructors representation is not clear. As pointed out earlier, the Andhra Mahila Sabha made the President of the Sirsilla Panchayat Samithi as the Chairman of the Project Level Committee. The Project Officer, Supervisor, some officials of block level administration are the members. The P L C of the Durga Sangh Seva Samaj consists of Convenor, Supervisor and two women members and the Extension Officer incharge of Education of Panchayat Samithi.

There is thus a variation in the composition of the P L Cs constituted by the agencies in the sample. As for the Project Level Committee (PLC) meetings, again going by agencywise, the PLC of BCT met at the beginning of every month.

A cursory glance at the agenda of the monthly meetings of various agencies in the sample revealed that a number of problems were brought to the notice of the P L C for a decision. These include (a) dropout problem ; (b) non-co-operation of village elite ; (c) non receipt of grant from the Government ; (d) trooping of children into adult education centres ; (e) absence of instructors without intimation ; (f) clash in timings of adult education centres and other developmental programmes of the agency ; (g) criteria for consideration of applicants who also happen to be learners for loans ; (h) non functioning of village level committees ; (i) indifference or non-co-operation of the developmental functionaries to visit adult education centres for giving lectures etc. ; (j) arrangements for inspections by the officials of the adult education directorate and other district officials ; (k) arranging lectures by the functionaries in-charge of agriculture, animal husbandry etc., within the agency, and other problems.

The usual procedure for conducting the meetings of PLC is first to listen to the instructor followed by the supervisor on various aspects of the programme mangement. On several occasions there was a difference of opinion and in such a situation the Chairman tried for a consensus. The methods of finding solution to the problem are through discussion, dialogue with the concerned and between the concerned.

As the Chairman of a P L C rightly summed up the "committee looked at each problem with an intention to solve it." Very often the patience of the Chairman was put to test. Placed as he was in a difficult situation, conducting meetings with a widely stratified members is "a tight rope to walk on." On the whole the P L C served the purpose for which it was created. An agency involved in diversified activities naturally confronts special problems of co-ordination which for that very reason may find solution easily. The organizers of the programme were once faced with the problem of finances. The second installment of the grant for running the programme was not released.[32] The P L C of that agency took a decision to divert the funds from other sources. The agency could have closed down all centres after five months and could have shifted the blame on the government, but the organisers observed that it would have dampened the enthusiasm of learners. Moreover it was feared that the other educational programmes of the agency may not succeed and secondly winding up a programme for lack of funds would impair the image of the agency. Thus, it can be seen that the P L C of one agency i.e., B C T was favourably situated to arrange co-ordination amongst its different activities. The village level committees of this agency however have not functioned to the extent the organisers desired.

Coming to CROSS as already stated the P L C was not as broad in its composition as was the case with B C T. Problems similar to B C T were faced by this agency also, except in one area. The local leaders have not co-operated much with the agency. The wide network of village sanghams are a constant source of tension between the agency and local level bureaucracy on the one hand and between the local leaders and the agency on the other. This agency too, sponsored several economic programmes like B C T. At the end of every month the meetings of the P L C were held and problems of adult education centres were brought to the notice of the Chairman through the supervisor. Solutions were worked out to overcome problems and efforts were made to avoid clash with the adult education centres activities and other activities of the agency. Criteria for the processing of applications for loans to banks was framed and guidelines were formulated. Project Level Committee (P L C) prepared a list of resource persons for lectures in adult education centres. Methods of motivating and attracting illiterate adults were discussed and measures were suggested to the instructors to sustain the interest of learners. The members of the P L C visited some centres and recorded their satisfaction on the progress. Thus the mechanism for achieving internal co-ordination is sound and produced the desired effect. But as far as external co-ordination is concerned the agency found it difficult to secure. The environment around the agency is hostile. Local elite to a large extent suspect the agency. According to reliable source the block level bureaucracy envies the agency for its initiative, boldness and result orientation. It was given to understand that some vested interests wrote letters to the Government urging it to stop the grants to CROSS for its anti-government activities. Pressures were brought or police to wind up even the agency. CROSS has some sort of a village level co-ordinating committees also and these are called village level sanghams.

As regards the operation of P L C of A M S in Sirsilla, as pointed out elsewhere it was headed by a local leader as Chairman. It may be recalled that the Andhra Mahila Sabha is not new to organizing literacy programmes. The investigator hoped that with its vast experience, this agency would run the programme more easily and effectively. However, this very agency started facing problems right from the beginning. The P L C has not laid down a proper criteria for location of adult education centres keeping in view the local conditions. With the result some centres had been shifted, closed down and re-opened. The policy guidelines on location of centres seemed to have been ignored.

The problems that arose in the implementation of the programme were not attended to. The P L C itself rarely met and naturally several problems of co-ordination emerged which called for higher policy direction. The Project Officer tried several times to make the P L C to meet regularly. When it met, the Chairman was always in a hurry to leave. Hence no proper discussion used to take place. The whole management of running 100 adult education centre fell on the Project Officer who, though had sufficient experience, was relatively young in age. In the absence of regular mechanism for co-ordinating the work, the programme could not be implemented effectively. The developmental functionaries have not shown any interest in the programme in spite of the fact that the President of Panchayat Samithi was associated with the programme. According to the Project Officer the Chairman is so indifferent that on one occasion he suggested to the project officer to take his signature on all papers/cheques once in four months so that the work did not suffer. Thus the P L C of the A M S largely remained on paper. As regards village level committees, A M S did not seem to have taken any initiative to organise them.

In the case of Durga Sangh Seva Samaj too, the investigator noticed the ineffectiveness of the PLC. The convenor of the committee is also the director of the agency. When enquired about the PLC he observed that the matters relating to the PLC are confidential and will not be revealed. The investigator through other sources was informed that the PLC met only once at the beginning of the programme. The non-functioning of the PLC has adversely affected the functioning of the programme. The major casualty of non-functioning of PLC was internal as well as external co-ordination. Issues like the criteria for recruitment to the instructor's post, whether it is desirable to recruit the retired teachers, the quality of the teaching material, location of centres, lighting facilities, the problems involved in opening adequate number of women centres, the problems with regard to arranging lectures by resource persons etc., should have come up before the PLC as in the case of other agencies. In the absence of this vital co-ordinating body the organizers were forced to look for ad-hoc measures to cope with exigencies which led to lot of dissatisfaction among learners as well as the instructional cadre. Thus the agency failed to take the advantage of an important body like the PLC.

Coordination with other Developmental Departments

As regards co-ordination with other developmental departments of the Government, the supervisors cited several reasons. Giving benefit of doubt to the government servants the supervisor of BCT and CROSS opined that the governmental functionaries did not have much time and the orders of the district collectors/director of adult education programme are not binding on them. The overburdened developmental bureaucracy hardly have any time to participate in adult education programme enthusiastically.

The supervisors of DSS and AMS stated that the block level functionaries wanted them to arrange conveyance to visit centres which they just could not do. The supervisor of AMS said that though his agency owned three imported two wheelers (gifted by Canadians) not even one was sent to the field in spite of several requests. When this question was put to the officials of the agency, they said that "the vehicles get spoiled if driven on dirty village roads" which left investigator to wonder as to the very purpose of keeping idle the vehicles at headquarters when the work is actually being executed in the field. The supervisor of the DSS said his agency did not have a vehicle.

The BCT, however, used its vehicles for bringing resource persons like block level officials. This enabled the officials to participate to some extent in the programme by giving occasional lectures and by answering several questions raised by learners. Presence of officials enthused learners to such an extent that they were feared to answer tough questions like the reasons for the administrative delay in processing their applications for loans etc. This trend in fact had produced a negative effect also on the involvement of officials as they felt that these centres had become a 'nuisance' to them and they stopped visiting on various excuses. This, however, does not mean that all officials felt shy to face learners.

With regard to co-ordination with other agencies implementing NAEP none of the project officers in charge of adult education centres directly under the government cared to visit centres under the voluntary agencies. Adult education programmes sponsored by the Government of Andhra Pradesh are going on in places close by to those operated by agencies. When the investigator enquired about it, the Project Officers of the Government replied that to visit all the 300 adult education centres directly under their jurisdiction is proving to be an uphill task and therefore the question of visiting centres under 'others' according to them was unimaginable.

The same trend is noticed more or less in case of all the agencies like Universities & Colleges, NSS, ICDS Schemes etc. The involvement of developmental functionaries as envisaged in policy statement (and in other documents subsequently released by the Government of India) too had not materialised to the extent desired. The reasons for their partial involvement were already discussed. With this let us move on to the systems of monitoring and evaluation.

Monitoring and Evaluation

One of the main functions of the supervisors is to ensure that they follow the reporting systems i.e. monthly and quarterly reports. All supervisors reported compliance with the instructions in this regard and all instructors sent the reports in time. It appeared that the formats for reporting too were lengthy. On this the superivisors felt that it should be smaller in size. Two out of four supervisors admitted that the instructors' reports did not exactly reflect the facts relating to daily attendance, dropouts etc. The position with regard to other two supervisors is interesting. They told the instructors that if they reported correct situation they would be rewarded and they would be punished for wrong figures. This seems to have led, at least to some extent, to correct reporting.

Job Satisfaction

All the supervisors have stated that they are satisfied with their jobs. The supervisors of BCT and CROSS said that a little more co-operation from the government would have made them much more satisfied.

The supervisor of AMS felt that the officials of his agency should pay more interest towards programme by visiting some adult education centres. On the whole all the supervisors observed that they derived a lot of satisfaction from their jobs.

General Impressions

All the supervisors opined that the success of the programme in terms of targets was commendable as they said that they could make at least 50-60 per cent of the enrolled literate. Most of them, however, are sceptical about success of other two components. Further, the supervisors of BCT felt that there were several limitations to put into operation functional and awareness components. To some extent, he viewed that the functional education component was attempted by admitting some learners in carpentry training centres but only after they completed ten month course. On awareness component he said it would take some more time.

All the supervisors have unanimously endorsed the view that the NAEP would succeed if more voluntary agencies are associated. They further felt that the progress though not a spectacular success, it definitely resulted in creation of a favourable environment as anticipated by policy makers.

Suggestion

The supervisor of BCT suggested that the present policy of extending education 'free of cost' to adult illiterates calls for a thorough review. The value of education according to the respondents will be realised only when the learner pays from his pocket. The government may supply all resource material like books etc., but the honorarium must at least be met by the adults out of contributions or else it is difficult to check the casual attitude of the illiterates.

Furthermore the supervisor suggested that government

must take into confidence the voluntary agencies which were given permission to implement adult education programme. It should create 'demand' for education by equalizing the qualification acquired by adult illiterate to seventh or fifth class.

The supervisors from other agencies in the sample suggested effective involvement of developmental functionaries of government. This gained currency owing to reports that teaching by an instructor continuously may lead to monotony and the lectures by "others" might arouse interest. The other suggestions include change in pattern as well as emphasis on training, modification in resource material, relaxation of procedures for obtaining grants and other financial assistance for carrying follow-up or post-literacy programmes, delegation of powers from the PLC to the supervisors to select the instructor, supply of audio-visual equipment free of cost by the Taluq Public Relations Officer etc., provision for vehicles for effective supervision.

An analysis of the role and functioning of the supervisors reveals that they have a fairly good grasp and understanding of the NAEP., all of them belong to the prescribed age group and the investigators noticed certain amount of commitment. Their dissatisfaction with the training programme has to be taken note of as it greatly helps them in appreciating their role as key level functionaries and directly contributes to increasing their effectiveness.

Sincere attempts by all the supervisors of all the agencies seemed to have been made to involve the developmental personnel at the block level but success in this regard varied. While the supervisor of the BCT because of his good rapport with block level personnel could involve at least some of them, the supervisor of DSS and AMS could not do much to involve them as the officials of their agencies themselves were not seemed to be aware of the benefits accruing from that. The limitations cited by the supervisors in imparting functional education and increasing awareness must be examined more deeply.

Inter-agency co-operation may yield better results in this regard. With regard to monitoring and evaluation the view of the supervisors that the instructor is overburdened with paper work merits serious consideration. The study also revealed as to how effective supervision depends on provision of conveyance facilities. Average number of visits by the supervisors belonging to two agencies in the sample to centres under their control are much higher than the case with other two. The fact that one agency got rhe vehicles and is not thinking of giving them to supervisors further reveals the agencies' belief in effective supervision. No doubt there may be more number of supervisors than vehicles. But the solution does not lie in keeping the vehicles idle. Moreover, it appears that it is not a difficult problem to tackle.

As regards co-ordination, the project level committees attached to each agency need to be activated. Instead of meeting only once in 5 months as was the case with a couple of agencies in the sample it should meet once in a month. Regular meetings of PLC's facilitate quick decision making pertaining to the project. The methods adopted by BCT for securing co-ordination appear to be more effective and hence deserve to be emulated by others in this regard.

After the discussion on the role, functions, problems of the instructors and supervisors of the adult education centres, we now turn to matters relating to the target group i.e., learners, dropouts and potential learners. In fact, any meaningful measurement of the impact of policy can be evaluated only with the responses gathered from the 'target' group.

NOTES AND REFERENCES

1. *Policy Statement on National Adult Education Programme*, Government of India, Ministry of Education and Social Welfare, New Delhi, 1978, p. 2.
2. Dimock & Dimock, *Public Administration* (New Delhi : Oxford University Press and India Book House Publishers, 1975), p. 258.
3. *Ibid.*, p. 258
4. Mohit Bhattacharya, *Public Administration* (Calcutta : World Press, 1981) p. 161.
5. *Ibid.* p. 161.

6. N A E P : *An Outline*, Government of India, Ministry of Education and Social Welfare, New Delhi, 1978, p. 16.
7. *Ibid.*
8. *Training of Instructors* in Training of Education Functionaries, No : 2, Directorate of Adult Education, Ministry of Education and Social Welfare, Government of India, New Delhi, 1980, p. 5.
9. *Methodology of Training* No : 1, Directorate of Adult Education, Ministry of Education and Social Welfare, Government of India, New Delhi, 1980, pp. 2-3.
10. *Ibid..*, p. 9.
11. Interview with project Officer B C T., Yellamanchili. The trainees too confirmed the novel methods employed by the agency.
12. He is one of the most dynamic instructors of the sample and showed remarkable talents in running the A E C. Not contented with restrictive connotation attributed to the Social Awareness Component of the programme, this instructor explained to his learners (majority of whom were agricultural labourers), the legal position with regard to the minimum wages. The learners after realising how they were being cheated, attempted to put up a tough posture on wage rate for a day. The powerful vested interests of the village elites thwarted their attempt to get the minimum wage by bringing lorry load of labourers from a neighbouring district. Recalling the incident the instructor bemoaned at the plight of the labourers and said that the situation was not ripe enough to emphasise the awareness component as it might adversely affect the interests of the learners.
13. Such offer like loans have had positive and negative effects also. A good number of learners no doubt were convinced that the agencies known very much for their help will not disappoint them. However, in some centres under CROSS, a few learners repeatedly asked the instructors to arrange for the promised loans. The agency has its own priorities. In spite of agency's best efforts to convince the learners regarding the loan position, some learners dropped out. An official of the agency commented that they had decided not to use loans as a motivational issue to attract learners as this had become an additional burden on them.
14. In Centres under D S S and A M S some learners complained that their agencies wre interested only to establish a Centre, appoint an instructor and wash off hands. Further, a few learners told the investigator "once they get grants from government without questions they seem to be little interested to solve real problems faced by us". A few learners after completionof course asked for certificates which the officials seems to have ruled out. This, they say, is the 'least' they expect from the agency.
15. The Director of Adult Education, Government of Andhra Pradesh recently told at a news Conference about the government's positive thinking on this. See The Hindu, Hyderabad, 16 April, 1985.

16. The objective of Farmers Functional Literacy was only to increase agricultural production using latest technology available. In N A E P propagation of the use of agricultural inventions is only one of its many dimensions. It fact it is considered much more broad based in concept and application than Farmers Functional Literacy programme.
17. Here again one comes across peculiar instances. Local leaders helped the organisers of A E P in securing accommodation for the centre in a school : or an electric connection in some areas. Such help was done only when the candidate they recommended was posted as instructor. Where the agency could not oblige the 'elite', troubles of all sorts arose. Learners were instigated to rebel against the instructor ; instructed not to cooperate ; frightening women learners, if they attended classes etc. The agencies have their own version to this. They say that if local leaders recommend good candidates they do not mind accommodating one or two. But the local leaders by and large are recommending candidates with less competence and if they are appointed, the reputation of the agency is bound to suffer. These instances only indicate the general difficulties faced by voluntary agencies in implementing programmes like adult education.
18. In some centres the local leaders gave lot of trouble to the instructors. An instructor was given a memo by his superior for his participation in the programme ostensibly at the instance of a local leader.
19. The honorarium for instructor was Rs. 50/- per month. In 1984 the Government of India enhanced it to Rs. 100/-.
20. Interveiw with instructors of the Durga Sangh Seva Samaj.
21. Training of Adult Education Functionaries, No. 3, *Training of Supervisors*, Director of Adult Education, the Author, New Delhi, p. 5.
22. *Ibid.*, p. 2.
23. *Ibid.*, p. 3, Also see Handbook for Adult Education Functionaries.
24. *Ibid.*, p. 7.
25. *Ibid.*, p. 6.
26. *Ibid.*, p. 6.
27. *Ibid.*, p. 6.
28. *Ibid.*, p. 6.
29. Directorate of Adult Education, Government of India, Handbook on "Training Programme for Adult Education Functionaries", New Delhi, 1978, p. 9.
30. Various names like Project Level Committee, N A E P Co-ordination Committee, Steering Committee. Project Co-ordination body are used to denote the agency for securing co-ordination of the adult education work by the agencies in the sample. After an examination of the functions and the instruments used for securing the co-ordination by the agencies in the sample, it was found that more or less similar functions are performed by the bodies created

by the agencies to attend to N A E P work. Hence, it has been decided to use P L C for clarity.

31. At the time of the application for grants, the agencies are expected to give a broad picture of Administrative Framework for implementing the N A E P. Some agencies have mentioned about the body for looking after the administration of the programme. The investigator culled the information from different sources.
32. The B C T got the second installment of the grant from the Government after more than a year of the conclusion of the programme. Recalling the incident, the Secretary of the B C T stated that they would never go for government help in this regard as they had "burnt their fingers once". This will reveal how the bureaucracy can effectively drive away an enthusiastic voluntary agency from participating in public policies.

5

Learners and Dropouts

The objective of the National Adult Education Programme is to educate illiterate adults. Education of an illiterate adult as conceived by the policy makers of National Adult Education Programme is intended not only to promote literacy but also to extend functional education and social awareness. The results of the programme are to be judged in terms of these three criteria : literacy, functional education and social awareness. The assessment of the performance of learners in this study therefore is in terms of ascertaining the level of literacy, functional education and social awareness attained by the learners. Besides learners, it also seeks to study the impact of the programme on dropouts and potential learners. It was felt that study of the opinions of the dropouts and potential learners is equally important in determining the overall impact of the programme.

As has already been pointed out earlier the study covers nineteen adult educatian centres. The sample includes 30 per cent of the learners enrolled at each centre which works out to 171. About 57 dropouts at the rate of 3 per adult education centre and 38 potential learners at the rate of 2 per adult education centre were selected.

Three separate interview schedules were prepared and presented to thc learners, the dropouts and the potential learners.[1] The schedule on the learners[2] sought to elicit information from the learners on various aspects of the programme besides their socio-economic background. The schedule on dropouts was intended to generate information pertaining not only to their socio-economic status, but also their reasons for withdrawing from the course and the conditions undcr wnich they rejoined the programme. And finally the schedule on potential learners[3] was prepared with a view to gauging their reactions to the programme, as also to get some insights into the process by which the agencies identified potential learners from amongst the eligible learners.

To facilitate presentation, this chapter has been divided into five sections. These are : (1) The socio-economic background of the learners, dropouts and potential learners. (2) The learners and their reasons for joining the Adult Education Centres. (3) The location and the organization of the Adult Education Centres. (4) The learners' reaction to the resource material, the method of instruction and the attitudes of instructors. (5) The reasons for the dropping out of learners and an analysis of the response from the potential learners.

1. Socio-economic background of the Learners, Dropouts and Potential Learners

In this section, it is proposed to study the socio-economic background of the learners, dropouts and the potential learners, who are the main target group of the programme.

Tables 18 to 21 present the socio-economic background. The main variables for the study are (i) caste, and sex, (ii) age, (iii) occupation and (iv) income.

(i) Caste and sex

In terms of cast it will be noticed from the above table that out of the total sample of 171 learners, as many as 88.30 per cent of the learners belong to the lower classes i.e., scheduled caste and backward classes. Among these sections, 49.12 per cent of the learners fall into the scheduled caste category and 39.18 per cent belong to the backward class. The percentage of forward classes is 11.70. Thus nearly 90 per cent of the learners in the sample belong to the lower classes. As one of the aims of the National Adult Education Programme is to reach the rural poor and those sections which suffer educational deprivation, the study shows that the programme has succeeded in reaching the intended target group to a more than substantial extent.

TABLE 18

Distribution of Caste and Sex among Learners, Dropouts and Potential Learners

Caste	Learners		Dropouts		Potential Learners	
	Male	Female	Male	Female	Male	Female
Scheduled Caste	65 (47.45)	19 (55.88)	23 (60.53)	8 (42.11)	10 (30.30)	3 (60.00)
Backward Classes	54 (39.42)	13 (38.24)	11 (28.95)	5 (26.32)	10 (30.30)	1 (20.00)
Forward Caste	18 (13.13)	2 (5.88)	4 (10.52)	5 (31.57)	13 (39.40)	1 (20.00)
Total	137 (100.00)	34 (100.00)	38 (100.00)	19 (100.00)	33 (100.00)	5 (100.00)

(Figures in parentheses indicate percentages)

Sex-wise too the results are encouraging. Among the scheduled caste learners in the sample, around 23 per cent are females and among the backward classes they constitute about 20 per cent. The response from the learners belonging to the forward class is relatively unfavourable. This may be due to the fact that these sections of the population do not prefer to join adult education centres as they have had some rudimentary education already. But, interestingly enough, there is also another reason which cannot but be taken into account. Some of the people from the forward castes have expressed the view in oral conversation that as programmes like these are likely to draw the backward classes and that, therefore, they would not like to join in. This is no doubt a typical instance of an elitist reaction.

Dropouts

Analysis of the data on dropouts[4] shows that the scheduled castes constitute about 54.39 per cent of the total dropouts in the sample. The backward classes account for 28.07 per cent followed by forward classes which is 17.54 per cent. The high dropout rate of the scheduled caste learners may be attributed to lack of motivation. The responses of the dropouts support this conclusion. This aspect of the problem will be highlighted in a greater detail later. The other reasons for dropouts from the programme are also dealt with in the later part of this chapter.

Potential Learners

Here again, about 63.16 per cent of the respondents belong to lower classes though when compared to the learners' sample the figure for the forward castes is slightly higher. The percentage of forward classes in this category is slightly higher. So the voluntary agencies have by and large succeeded in attracting illiterates belonging to backward sections.

Age

The National Adult Education Programme (NAEP) is intended mainly for those people who are in the age group of 15-35 years. The interview schedules canvassed for learners, dropouts and potential learners include a question about their age with a view to finding out whether the objective of making available the AEP to the target group is achieved or not. The following table reveals the age-wise distribution of the respondents.

An analysis of the age of the first category of respondents i.e., learners shows that about 74 per cent male learners and about 56 per cent female learners fall in the age group of 15-35 years. Thus a majority of learners (70 per cent) belong to this intended target group which is in conformity with the policy objectives of the National Adult Education Programme.[5]

TABLE 19

Age-wise Distribution of Learners, Dropouts and Potential Learners

Age Group in years	Learners Male	Learners Female	Dropouts Male	Dropouts Female	Potential Learner Male	Potential Learner Female
14 or less	16 (11.68)	10 (29.41)	3 (7.89)	—	—	—
15—20	27 (19.71)	10 (29.41)	16 (42.12)	10 (52.63)	6 (18.18)	2 (40.00)
21—25	35 (25.55)	5 (14.71)	7 (18.42)	4 (21.05)	11 (33.33)	3 (40.00)
26—30	20 (14.60)	2 (5.88)	6 (15.79)	4 (21.05)	13 (39.39)	1 (20.00)
31—35	19 (13.86)	2 (5.88)	3 (7.89)	1 (5.27)	3 (9.10)	—
36 and above	20 (14.60)	5 (14.71)	3 (7.89)	—	—	—
Total	137 (100.00)	34 (100.00)	38 (100.00)	19 (100.00)	33 (100.00)	5 (100.00)

(Figures in the parentheses indicate percentages)

However, it is interesting to find that while the programme is intended to cover those in the age group of 15-35 years, 26 per cent of males and 44 per cent of the females of the sample fall outside the intended target group. This fact has a bearing on the adequacy or efficacy of the 'target group survey' supposed to have been conducted by the agencies running the programme. These agencies of course, have undertaken in order to identify those who come under this prescribed age group. Further they canvassed among those so identified to join the programme. Those who expressed a desire to join the programme were identified as potential learners. As it is an established fact that an overwhelmingly large sections of the village population in this age group is illiterate the members that are eligible for the programme are bound to be much more than those who could be covered by the programme. In other words, those that are enrolled as learners will necessarily be a small percentage of the eligible learners and the agency surveys were supposed to identify potential learners from among the eligible learners to be inducted as learners. The point is that as quite a few people in the sample do not fall in the eligible learners category, it would appear as though the identification of potential learners was not strictly made from the eligible learners category. This point is further corroborated from the information gathered from the responses of potential learners. No doubt, some potential learners have not joined the programme for various reasons even though canvassed to do so. It was also noticed that there were some eligible learners who informed the rcsearcher that they were not approached at all. Had the survey by voluntary agencies been more exhaustive some more learners could have been identified to fill the places which were actually filled by those falling outside the intended age group as is shown in the sample. The induction of those falling outside the age group not only prevented some eligible learners from coming in, but also raised certain specific problems by the admission of those above and below the age group.[6]

Coming back to the main table the following points are worth noting. The respondents in the sample i.e. the learners, the dropouts and the potential learners fall into different age-groups. About 45.25 per cent male learners and 44.12 per cent female learners figure in the 15-25 age group. Both male and female learners of this age group thus constitute about 45.03 per cent of the sample for this age group. About 28.47 per cent male learners and about 11.76 per cent female learners figure in the 26-35 age group thereby constituting 25.15 per cent of the total sample of this age group. Thus one can make an interesting observation that younger people are attracted to this programme.

Occupation

An analysis of the occupational background of the three kinds of respondents is attempted in this section to understand which occupational group of respondents is represented more, and what the pattern of occupational distribution is. The details are presented below.

TABLE 20

Occupational Distribution of Learners, Dropouts and Potential Learners

Occupation	Learners		Dropouts		Potential Learners	
	Male	Female	Male	Female	Male	Female
Agricultural Labour	54 (39.42)	27 (79.42)	20 (52.63)	13 (68.43)	21 (63.64)	3 (60.00)
Small Farmers	32 (23.36)	2 (5.88)	5 (13.16)	1 (5.26)	5 (15.15)	— —
Marginal Farmers	7 (5.11)	— (—)	2 (5.26)	— —	1 (3.03)	— —
Large Farmers	1 (0.73)	—	—	—	—	—
Non-Agricultural Labour	17 (12.41)	2 (5.88)	7 (18.42)	3 (15.79)	4 (12.12)	1 (20.00)
Rural Artisans	5 (3.65)	1 (2.94)	3 (7.89)	1 (5.26)	1 (3.03)	— —
Others	21 (15.32)	2 (5.88)	1 (2.64)	1 (5.26)	1 (3.03)	1 (20.00)
Total	137 (100.00)	34 (100,00)	38 (100.00)	19 100.00)	33 (100.00)	5 (100.00)

(Figures in parnetheses indicate percentages)

The table brings out an interesting fact that a majority of learners, dropouts and potential learners i.e., approximately 48, 50, and 63 per cent respectively belong to agricultural labour. Small farmers, the next category of respondents, constitute about 20 per cent among the learners, 11 per cent in the dropouts and nearly 14 per cent among the potential learners. The other occupations, barring large farmers are more or less evenly distributed. The largest number of learners is from the agricultural labour category who seem to have shown a keen interest.

The reasons for a large number of dropouts from the said category are analysed elsewhere in this chapter. Significantly, a lesser number of rural artisans and non-agricultural labour were attracted to this programme and a considerable number then dropped out.

Income-wise distribution

The income-wise distribution of the learners, dropouts and potential learners is also investigated to study which income group has evinced greater interest in the programme. The details of the income distribution of the three categories of respondents is presented in Table 21.

A major percentage of the learners (51-46 per cent) belong to Rs. 1501-2500 income group. Female learners, constitute about 64.71 per cent and male learners constitute 48.18 per cent of the sample. About 23 per cent of the male learners, and about 21 per cent of female learners fall in Rs. 501-1500 income bracket.

TABLE 21

Income-wise Distribution of Learners, Dropouts and Potential Learners

Income per annum	Learners		Dropouts		Potential Learners	
	Male	Female	Male	Female	Male	Female
501-1500	32 (23.36)	7 (20.59)	16 (42.11)	9 (47.37)	13 (39.39)	3 (60.00)
1501-2500	66 (48.18)	22 (64.71)	12 (31.57)	5 (26.32)	13 (39.39)	2 (40.00)
2501-3500	26 (18.98)	4 (11.76)	5 (13.16)	3 (15.79)	7 (21.22)	— —
3501-4500	5 (3.65)	1 (2.94)	6 (13.16)	2 (20.52)	—	—
4501-5500	1 (0.73)	—	—	—	—	—
5501—and	7 (5.10)	—	—	—	—	—
Total	137 (100.00)	34 (100.00)	38 (100.00)	19 (100.00)	33 (100.00)	5 (100.00)

(Figures in the parentheses indicate percentages)

Coming to the dropouts, a majority of them (44 per cent) belong to the Rs. 501-1500 income group while about 29.82 per cent fall in the Rs. 501-2500 income group. The rest of the learners are more or less evenly distributed in the higher income brackets. As far as potential learners are concerned, 42.10 per cent belong to the Rs. 501-1500 income range while 40 per cent fall in the Rs. 1501-2500 category.

It is interesting to observe that about 73 per cent of the learners, 73.68 of the dropouts and 81.57 per cent of the potential learners fall in the Rs. 501-1550 which is lowest income group. This group predominantly consists of marginal farmers and agricultural labourers. As can be observed from the table, the dropouts are in a higher percentage amongst the Rs. 501-1500 group. Probably this is accountable due to the absence of effective motivational techniques on the part of the agencies. Yet, there are other explanations also. The percentage of dropouts shows a declining trend as the income grows. This may be due to the fact that in general people try to concentrate on education as their economic status improves. Data on potential learners confirms the trend of the respondents in the villages. Their reasons for not joining are dealt with separately.

Former Literacy Level

Another important variable considered for measuring the interest of respondents is their earlier literacy level. The policy planners of the National Adult Eduaation Programme visualised that "illiterates", as the term literally suggests, are the priority and therefore the focus should be on them. With a view to knowing whether the agencies satisfied the policy directive that total "illiterates" should be given priority and preference in enrolment, the schedules administered on the learners carry a question to find out whether they attended a school or studied privately before their joining in an adult education centres. Likewise the schedules on dropouts and potential learners too were questioned whether they were literates or illiterates. (For the purposes of the present analysis a literate is one who studied upto the primary level either in school or privately). The details are presented below:

TABLE 22

Distribution of Learners, Dropouts, Potential Learners, according to the earlier literacy level

Literacy	Learners		Dropouts		Potential Learners	
	Male	Female	Male	Female	Male	Female
Illiterates	90 (65.69)	30 (88.24)	30 (78.95)	16 (84.21)	32 (96.97)	5 (100.00)
Literates	47 (34.31)	4 (11.76)	8 (21.05)	3 (15.79)	1 (3.03)	—
Total	137 (100.00)	34 (100.00)	38 (100.00)	19 (100.00)	33 (100.00)	5 (100.00)

(Figures in the parentheses indicate the percentage)

It will be observed from the table that nearly 70 per cent of the learners enrolled are total illiterates, which means that the voluntary agencies have by and large acceded to the policy directive of giving priority to total illiterates. The fact that about 30 per cent of learners who have had some level of literacy were given admission confirms the limitations of the survey conducted by the agencies. As can be noticed from the table the dropout rate among the illiterates is as much as 80 per cent. About 97 per cent of the potential learners in the sample are "illiterates".

A general analysis of the socio-economic background of learners, dropouts and potential learners discussed above help us in deriving a few more inferences.

(1) The programme implemented through agencies in the sample did attract a large number of adult illiterates belonging to priority groups like scheduled castes and backward classes.

(2) The agencies have, by and large, satisfied the policy objective of attracting the target group of learners in the age group of 15-35 years though more attention on the survey would have resulted in attracting larger numbers in this group.

(3) The proportion of dropouts in the 15-35 age group is higher, suggesting that there were drawbacks in the methods of motivating them to stay for the 10 month duration.

(4) The agencies also broadly followed the objective of giving preference to lower income groups in enrolment in the adult education centres.

(5) The record of the earlier literacy level of learners and drop-outs suggests that the agencies, to a large extent enrolled learners with no literacy level, although much needs to be done in perfecting the survey method adopted by the agencies.

Section II

The Learners and their reasons for joining A E Cs

The socio-economic background of the learners, dropouts and potential learners has been analysed to make a comparative study of various caste and income groups that were attracted to the programme. In this section the reasons given by the learners for joining the Adult Education Centres are analysed. These reasons are considered as important for measuring the level of interest of those who attended the programme. Table 23 prcsents the reasons given by the learners for joining the Adult Education Centres.

TABLE 23

Reasons for joining A E C by Learners

(in percentages)

Reasons	AMS	BCT	CROSS	DSS
N=	90	27	27	27
1. To learn signatures	75	46	50	50
2. To be able to read and write	60	35	40	60
3. To be able to identify Bus names	80	75	60	70
4. To be able to identify Cinema names	85	90	80	85
5. To learn about agriculture	25	20	50	30
6. To recognize rates in shop	50	20	25	45
7. Helpful at new places	15	10	30	45
8. To understand the contents of pronotes.	55	65	62	40
9. To gain general awareness	5	15	15	7
10. To be able to estimate wages	15	10	35	45

However, it should be kept in mind that the reasons stated by learners need not be considered as their 'felt needs'. It is possible to change the response pattern as well as the very reasons by providing an appropriate mix of the activities and learning experiences in the centres. For example, if the functional education component is strengthened by giving them training in some trades like carpentry, masonry or weaving, incorporating the latest methods, there would have been an appreciable change in the response pattern. Further, it can be seen that reasons are closely related to the desire to learn to read and write, acquire numeracy, and increase general knowledge. For example, 'to be able to read and write' has been given as the reason by about 50 per cent of the learners in the centres run by all the four agencies. Similarly, 'able to learn numeracy' constitutes the motivation of 59 per cent to 47 per cent of the learners. Knowledge about new farming techniques seems to be the factor motivating 51 per cent of 39 per cent of the learners while a need to get familiar with weights and measures is given as the reason inspiring about 50 per cent of the learners (52 to 42) to join the course. These figures no doubt indicate an encouraging trend.

But what is strange is that such other 'odd' reasons like 'being able to identify cinema names' too, motivated a much larger percentage of learners (70 to 62) to join the course. The desire to be able to identify buses and find out their destination also figures as a reason for 63 to 47 per cent of the learners. Learning to put their signature is another reason given by a relatively high number of learners 61 to 51 per cent. Perhaps this reflects the need for literacy arising out of involvement in litigation which is rampant in rural areas. The village peoplc are gullible and are often caught up in situations involving forgeries and some other malpractices. Incidentally, the phenomenal increase in the incidents of writing applications for loans, house sites and various other 'opportunities' now brought to the rural poor as part of the package on development may also account for this urge to learn to put their signature instead of the proverbial 'left hand thumb impression' which had become the badge of illiteracy in India.

In contrast, reasons relating to the acquisition of functional knowledge appear to motivate less. Thus, 'learning a trade' received a positive response only from 30 to 18 per cent of the learners. 'Knowing about animal husbandry' gets the least score, a mere 15 to 0 per cent. It is equally disheartening to know that very fcw, (15 to 0 per cent), are motivated by the desire to increase their general knowledge.

Awareness about the existence of A E C

Learners' awareness about the Adult Education Centre is one of the variables that generally suggests the flow of communication in rural areas. It is also important to study the sources of awareness in order to know how communication reaches the beneficiaries. A study of the dissemination of information and the people who spread it would also throw light on the capability of agencies to mobilize different sections of people and use them for positive purposes. In this section sources of awareness have been identified and the contribution of each source is empirically tested, the details of which analysis are given in be following Table.

TABLE 24

Awareness about the existence of Adult Education Centres

Agency	Sources				
	Friends	Instructors	Elite	Others	Total
Andhra Mahila Sabha (A M S)	20 (22.22)	41 (45.55)	11 (12.23)	18 (20.00)	90 (100.00)
Bhagavathula Charitable Trust (B C T)	3 (11.11)	14 (51.86)	6 (22.22)	4 (14.81)	27 (100.00)
Comprehensive Rural Operations Service Society (CROSS)	2 (7.40)	10 (37.04)	8 (29.63)	7 (25.93)	27 (100.00)
Durga Sangh Seva Samaj (D S S)	4 (14.81)	13 (48.15)	7 (25.93)	3 (11.11)	27 (100.00)

(Figures in parentheses indicate percentages)

A close observation of the Table reveals that the instructors and the 'elite' are the most important sources who have given publicity to the starting of Adult Education Centres. Further, an analysis of awareness agencywise, reveals that 45.55 per cent of the instructors in the centres run by A M S took up the responsiblity of informing the illiterate adults about the existence of Adult Education Centres. In the case of other agencies in the sample the major burden of campaigning about adult education centres fell on the instructors. The other sources include block officials, general publicity like drum beat methods in some villages. The learners themselves feel that information about the existence of the centres was publicized adequately through several sources.

Section III

Location and Organization of Adult Education Centres

Education under NAEP takes place in what is called Adult Education Centre (A E C). Although it is non-formal in one sense, adult education has some formal structure. Classes are held in a particular place for a specified period and a specified content is taught. Thus adult education requires certain physical facilities such as a suitable place for holding the classes.

TABLE 25

Location of Adult Education Centres

(in percentages)

Agency	School	Temple	Other Public place	Open space	Instructor House	Private House
Andhra Mahila Sabha	20	—	20	10	30	20
Bhagavathula Charitable Trust	—	34	33	—	33	—
Comprehensive Rural Operations Service Society	—	—	—	—	67	33
Durga Sangh Seva Samaj	34	—	—	—	33	34

As can be seen from the table a considerable number of the Adult Education Centres in the sample (37per cent) were run in the instructors' houses. About 21 per cent are located in private premises. The rest are evenly distributed among various other places like schools, temples, open and other public places. Some learners felt that the location of Adult Education Centre at the instructors' houses may not be very convenient to them, but temples, private houses, open places and other places, in their opinion, may not provide a conducive atmosphere either to run adult education centres. General inhibitions and reservations of adults to a particular place other than a public place will have a negative impact on their attendance.[7]

Illumination and Seating arrangement at A E Cs

Regarding physical facilities made available at the Centres out of 19 adult education centres nearly 8 had classes in the evening or late night which had electric lights, while kerosene lamps were used in the rest of the centres. As many as 16 adult education centres, the learners reported, had no special seating arrangements. Learners in these adult education centres reported that they squatted on the ground. Further the learners reported that only a few adult education centres were provided with durrie mats or benches for this purpose.

Distance

Adult Education Centres in the sample are located at different places. The suitability of a place for conducting adult education classes depends on how the learners feel about the convenience of the place. The location of the Adult Education Centre should be a place which is central to the village. Most of the learners (81 per cent) considered the distance between the Adult Education centre and their houses to be minimal. However, it will be interesting to note that 18 per cent of the learners complained that because of the distance involved, the location of the adult education centre was not convenient to them. Further, a good number of learners also complained about some inadequacies in the adult education centres like space, lighting and the problem of noise.

Attendance

One of the major tasks involved in running an adult education centre is to ensure the regular attendance of learners. The objectives of the national adult education programme cannot be realized unless a majority of the learners enrolled attend adult education centres regularly. The schedule canvassed for learners includes a question whether they have attended the classes regularly or not. In order to establish the veracity of the information given by the learners, the attendance registers maintained by the instructors were verified. The following table gives the general pattern of agency-wise attendance as gathered from the registers made available.

TABLE 26*

Average Daily Attendance—Agencywise

Sl. No.	Agency	Average daily attendance	Percentage
1	Andhra Mahila Sabha	25	83.33
2	Bhagavathula Charitable Trust	21	70.00
3	Comprehensive Rural Operations Service Society	22	73.33
4	Durga Sangh Seva Samaj	26	86.66

* Culled from the records maintained by the Instructors.

An overwhelming majority of learners in the sample (84 per cent) said they had regularly attended the adult education centre.

Some said that they could not attend regularly owing to a number of reasons like being busy with the peak agricultural session, domestic problems, health problems, the difficulty of going daily to a far off place for work, fatigue etc.

The response given by a majority of the learners regarding their attendance was verified with the help of registers provided by the instructors. As can be seen from the table the average attendance of learners ranged from 21 to 26 per day. The highest average attendance was recorded in centres under Durga Sangh Seva Samaj. In other centres the recorded attendance varies between 21 to 25 learners per centre. In terms of percentage nearly 87 per cent of learners are reported to have attended regularly in the centres run by D S S. The attendance in other centres varies between 70 and 83 per cent.

Yet this could not be the whole story regarding the attendance. During the field work the researcher detected that the learners' regularity as reported by them personally was not totally reliable. There are some indications of manipulation of the attendance register in some of the adult education centres. The register would show that an adult education centre had completed the stipulated 10 month period while, as a matter of fact, some centres were closed before the end of the prescribed period,[8] and in fact some were closed down although temporarily. Of course, the possibility of manipulation of registers and evidence of it in a few cases should not lead to the conclusion that the entire data collected from the register viz. the information on the duration of the adult education centre, actual number of classes held, genuineness of the list attendance learners are unreliable.

Section IV

Learners' reaction to the Learning Material, Method of Instruction and Instructors

The response of the learners to the material supplied, their opinion about the method of instruction, and their general assessment of the instructor, their achievement in literacy and their recapitulation of various topics discussed at the Adult Education Centres are studied in this section.

The agencies are expected to supply to all the learners in an adult education centre a slate, printed books, a work book, pencils and slate pencils and other material. The schedule tried to elicit responses on whether the learners in the sample received the reading/study material. The following table gives details about the material supplied to the learners in various adult education centres.

TABLE 27

Supply of Teaching/Learning Material as stated by Learners

(in percentages)

Sl. No.	Agency	Slates	Books	Note books	Pencils	Slate Pencils	Other
1	A M S	61	62	29	38	61	18
2	B C T	69	61	26	42	67	16
3	CROSS	62	57	17	—	65	14
4	D S S	54	51	15	32	56	17

More than half of the learners in the sample reported the receipt of the slates, the first item usually supplied to the learners. Regarding books, about 62 per cent of the learners enrolled in centres organized by Andhra Mahila Sabha reported receipt of the books, while 61 per cent of learners registered in the adult education centre conducted by the Bhagavathula Charitable Trust confirmed the receipt of books. Interestingly enough only a half of the learners in the sample received books in the centres run by the Durga Sangh Seva Samaj.

An inter-agency comparison of the other material supplied to the learners reveals that 67 to 56 per cent learners in the sample reported that they had received slate pencils, 26-15 per cent learners were given work books and 42-32 per cent got pencils. Except B C T and C R O S S which supplied other material like maps, posters etc. to the Adult Education Centre, the other two agencies have not done anything.

Thus a good number of the learners in the sample got the learning material. An interesting observation here is that the agencies do not seem to have geared up themselves to implement the programme. While a good percentage of learners in the sample complained that learning material was not supplied to them because the instructors had not received them in sufficient number, the agencies when asked to clarify this fact brushed aside the complaint and preferred to throw the blame on learners for giving away the printed and other material to their children. However, one agency admitted the lapses in the distribution of material to the learners and an official of

the agency told the researcher that these lapses are bound to take place in the first year of the programme. As the agency gains experience it would try to rectify its defects. There is some element of truth in the agencies' disatisfaction with the learners regarding learning material. In some of the adult education centres in Yellamananchili block those learners who got themselves enrolled got the material but a few of them dropped out and fresh learers were enrolled to fill the vacancies. The newly enrolled were not given printed material for obvious reasons. The other material like slates, slate pencils etc. is made available to them with the help of local community. The expenditure on printed and other material is continuously escalating and there is little financial leeway for the agencies to divert money for the material from other sources.

An assessment of the actual achievement of the learners would also provide an interesting comment upon the impact of the method of instruction employed. The literacy levels achieved by the learners were assessed by actual testing. For assessing the level of literacy achieved about 12 categories were identified. They include : (a) writing sentences ; (b) reading words ; (c) writing words ; (d) reading sentences ; (e) writing sentences ; (f) identifying numbers ; (g) adding single digits ; (h) subtracting single digits ; (i) multiplying and division of single digits ; (j) addition of two digits ; (k) subtraction of two digits ; and (l) multiplication and division of two digits.

The method of testing was however not standardized i.e. no standard technique, materials or methods were used. For testing, reading and writing abilities the primers supplied by the respective agencies to the learners were used. Depending on the type of test in reading and writing the words/sentences were picked up and the learner was asked to read them. Similarly the learners were given a piece of paper and were asked to write words/sentences. In some cases the learner's signature was taken as a test to assess his level of achievement in writing. Although there were instances of learners getting diffident, there were quite a few learners who showed a keen interest in answering the questions. Often, the testing went beyond the material supplied to the learners. In some cases the vernacular newspapers which the investigator carried with him were used to assess the achievement level of the learners in literacy.

The percentage of learners falling under different levels of achievement against each category are presented in Table 28. For each category again the responses are divided into three levels of achievement i.e. (i) all wrong, (ii) slow and partially correct and (iii) quick and all correct answers. Literacy here is taken in the conventional sense of skills in reading, writing and arithmetic. Separate tests were given to the learners for assessing their skills in reading, writing and elementary arithmetic skills. It was thought that a sort of a three category division is regarded as good enough to rank achievement of the learners, though more sophisticated techniques could have yielded even more precise indicators.

A majority of the learners (57.8 to 79 per cent) have acquired the ability to identify the Telugu (regional language) alphabet. It can be seen from the Table 28 that a good number of learners have also acquired the ability to read and write the words. We notice a fall in the percentage of adults who reported achievement of ability in reading and writing sentences (16.2—49 per cent). But as far as identifying numbers is concerned a good high percentage of learners (77.9—84.9) have achieved it.

Further an inter-agency comparison in reading and writing abilities of the learners would reveal that learners in B C T are better placed than others. An impressive percentage (79 per cent) of learners achieved ability to identify words, alphabet followed by those registered in centres under CROSS. Compared to B C T and CROSS the learners under D S S did not do well. Only 57.8 per cent could identify words while a much less percentage (24) could write words. Perhaps, this may be due to ineffective instruction in centres under their jurisdiction.

An assessment of the learners' achievement in literacy presented above therefore brings to light the relative importance each agency had given to the there R's (Reading, Writing and Arithmetic). An attempt will be made now to present the opinions of the learners on the topics that were taught to them besides literacy. Details about the topics discussed by various people besides instructors are given in the Table 29.

TABLE 28

Literacy Levels Achieved by the Learners

(in percentages)

Sl. No.	Type of Test	Andhra Mahila Sabha			Bhagavathula Charitable Trust			Comprehensive Rural Operations Service Society			Durga Sangh Seva Samaj		
		All wrong	Slow and partially correct	Fast and all correct	All wrong	Slow and partially correct	Fast and all correct	All wrong	Slow & Partially correct	Fast and all correct	All wrong	Slow and partialiy correct	Fast and all correct
1	Identifying Alphabet	2.9	24.2	72.9	1.8	19.2	79	1.9	19.1	79	3.6	38.6	57.8
2	Reading words	2.4	36.9	60.7	2.1	24.6	73.3	1.7	22.9	75.4	3.9	48.7	47.4
3	Writing words	25.7	48.3	26.0	19.8	42.1	38.1	18.9	46	35.1	22.2	46.8	24
4	Beading sentence	11.1	49.4	39.5	9.8	41.2	49	8.1	45.1	46.8	12.1	59.2	28.7
5	Writing sentence	26.12	48,12	25.8	2I,9	42.1	36	29.2	39.5	31.3	31.2	52.6	16.2

6 Identifying numbers	4.8	15.6	79.6	3.1	12.2	84.6	3.4	11.7	84.9	4	18.1	77.9
7 Adding single digits	72	26.3	1.7	59	38.1	2.1	63	34.3	2.7	76	2.8	1.2
8 Subtracting single digits	78.1	21.2	0.7	65	32.9	2.1	67.1	31.2	1.7	79.1	20.2	0.7
9 Multiplication and division of single digits	72.7	26.1	1.2	66.1	32.3	1.6	67.1	32.7	0.2	76.9	22.1	1
10 Addition of two digits	76.2	22.6	1.2	67.2	30.5	2.2	69.2	28.6	2.2	79.9	19.1	1
11 Substraction of two digits	78.1	20.7	1.2	70.1	27.8	2.1	69.9	27.8	2.3	79.9	19	1.1
12 Multiplication and division of two digits	76.8	21.6	1.6	69.7	28.2	2.1	70.1	27.6	2.3	82	16.9	1.1

As can be seen from the table a majority of the learners in the sample (72—50 per cent) reported that they were taught health and sanitation. Agriculture, which is the primary occupation of a majority of respondents, appears to have received its due share as a considerable number of learners reported its coverage in the Adult Education Centres (39-56 per cent). A good number of (30-50 per cent) learners further reported that discussion about minimum wages was one of the topics taken up in Adult Education Centres which aimed at educating them on the prevailing laws about the minimum wage. The inter-agency comparison would reveal that more learners enrolled under 'CROSS' reported the coverage than those under other agencies.

TABLE 29

Percentage of learners reporting about the topics taught at Adult Education Centres

Sl. No.	Subject	AMS N=90	SDS N=27	CROSS N=27	BCT N—27
1	Alphabet	80	72	74	60
2	About the village	40	35	30	45
3	Panchayat Institution	—	25	50	35
4	Agriculture	45	39	51	56
5	Animal husbandry	45	15	35	17
6	Health & Sanitation	72	64	56	50
7	Minimum wages to agricultural labour	30	35	50	47
8	Democracy	—	—	20	31
9	Family Planning	45	22	43	44
10	National Integration	50	18	46	31
11	Miscellaneous	48	40	31	38

(Percentages do not add up to 100 as respondents gave more than one answer)

It is interesting to observe from the table that not a single learner under Andhra Mahila Sabha reported coverage about the Panchayati Raj institutions which are the major implementors of rural development programmes. About 25 to 50 per cent of learners in Centres run by other agencies reported that Panchayati Raj was taught in their respective Centres. Two agencies (A M S and D S S) did not seem to have dealt with anything to do with democracy. The subject of Family Planning however received its fair share (22.44 per cent). Some learners also got information on national integration.

Thus the above analysis of topics dealt within Adult Education Centres as reported by learners help us in drawing two inferences : (1) The agencies have, by and large, given importance to the literacy component of the programme (60-80 per cent) rather than to the other components. Though the learners reported the coverage of topics under functional education (agriculture, animal husbandry) and social awareness, we are not sure as to how much they internalized since there is no report on this from the learners. The researcher also noticed some confusion in the understanding of the instructors, supervisors about the concepts like functional education and social awareness. Functional education is understood by instructors to be a component which emphasises the increase of production. Awareness building as contemplated by the policy makers in much more difficult in rural areas as any move towards it would be viewed with suspicion by the entrenched elite sections of the society. The learners reported that though they were told about latest metdods in agriculture they were not in a position to experiment with these now. Further, because of relatively high investment need and technical knowhow, functional education is not restricted to a narrow connotation. It ought to be used to stand for that knowledge which helps a larner to solve the day to day problems faced by him. With the help of the knowledge he acquires through the adult education centre, he should be able to function better in life.

A resourceful and enthusiastic instructor would facilitate the success of the National Adult Education Programme. Keeping this in view learners were asked to give their opinion about their respective instructors. The response was categorised below.

TABLE 30

Learners' Opinion about Instructors

Opinion Agency	Good Teacher	Old Man	Cannot explain the lesson	Failure to control	Rigid	Irregular	Others
A M S	34.5	—	52.6	49.1	10.6	12.12	29.6
B C T	69.0	—	21.6	—	5.4	17.8	16.8
CROSS	56.8	10.4	27.4	—	19.8	19.8	30.6
D S S	23.4	60.6	68.8	59.1	21.6	14.14	31.6

As can be seen from the Table 30, a good majority of respondents (69.0) enrolled in centres under B C T rated their instructors as 'good' followed by learners in centres run by CROSS (56.8 per cent). But the learners registered in centres under Andhra Mahila Sabha and Durga Sangh Seva Samaj seemed to have been dissatisfied with their instructors.

A considerable number of learners (52.6 per cent) in centres under Andhra Mahila Sabha categorically expressed an opinion that their instructors did not have the capacity to teach them properly. Some of them (49.1 per cent) have admitted the instructors' failure to even control them. A fair number (12.12 per cent) cited instances of the irregular attendance of the instructors. Similarly the learners enrolled in Adult Education Centres under Durga Sangh Seva Samaj also expressed their opinions on the limited ability of their instructors (68.8 per cent), lack of control on them (59.1 per cent) and irregularity in attendance (14 per cent). A good majority in these centres attributed their failure to benefit from the adult education centre due to the 'old age' of these instructors.

Thus the opinions of the learners about their respective instructors gives us a broad picture about the type of instructors attracted to this programme. The fact that the instructors chosen by two agencies B C T and CROSS have been favourably rated by the learners, taken together with the fact that these instructors appointed by the agencies are relatively young confirms the view that in the choice of instructors in future, unless the youth are given preference in recruitment as instructors, the learners will not get the necessary enthusiasm and even dropout. As stated elsewhere the Durga Sangh Seva Samaj had appointed only teachers (either retired or in service). While the two retired teachers could not win the confidence of the target group the third instructor proved an asset to the agency. The fact that he mobilized a good section of learners and even organized a type of revolt in pressing for an increase in the wages for the agricultural labourers, to an extent, indicates the rapport and confidence that young and enthusiastic instructors could establish vis-a-vis the learners.

Of the three agencies only B C T and CROSS which have some base in their respective areas of operation could succeed to some extent in mobilizing and motivating a large number of illiterates to attend Adult Education Centres. They have one advantage which the other two agencies do not have i.e. economic programmes in the villages.

Thus the analysis of various factors connected with the National Adult Education Programme reveal that programme is in need of certain modifications. Learners are the right judges to measure the success of the programme. Keeping this in view the respondents in the sample were asked to give their suggestions to increase the effectiveness of the programme. The responses are categorized agencywise. Several suggestions were made by them which are presented in the following table.

A majority of the learners (62—69.6 per cent) opined that if some economic incentives were offered there would be a greater possibility of the programme being a success. Flexibility in timings of the Centres (31—26.8 per cent), good lighting facilities (32.6—25 per cent), display of maps and charts (23—20.6 per cent), provision for audio and visual aids in the centres (31—19 per cent), regular supply of study material (40-14.6 per cent), extension of the duration of the programme from 20 months to 2 or 3 years (35—14.8 per cent), changes in the curriculum (27.4—7.6), increasing the functional education component (14.3—6.8) are some other important suggestions made.

TABLE 31

Suggestions given by Learners for the success of the Programmes—Agencywise

(in Percentages)

Sl. No.	Suggestions	AMS	BCT	CROSS	DSS
1.	Economic incentives to learners	62.6	65.9	69.6	68.8
2.	Flexibility in timings	29.7	26.8	31.4	30.7
3.	Good lighting facilities	25.0	27.6	30.8	32.6
4.	More about functional education	—	14.3	6.8	—
5.	Provide radio, T.V. etc.	31	30	29	19
6.	Regular supply of study material	29.1	—	14.6	40.3
7.	Centres should not be closed after 10 months	14.8	27.2	35.1	—
8.	Own building	7.8	17.4	16.8	15.3
9.	Supply of maps and Charts	22.1	20.6	20.4	23.2
10.	Change in curriculum	10.1	7.6	21.2	27.4
11.	Good instructor	11.4	3.6	10.8	29.8
12.	No suggestions	20	18	24	31

(Percentages do not add up to 100 because of multiple answers by the respondents)

Suggestions such as economic incentives indicate the general condition of poverty in which a majority of the rural poor are subjected to and also perhaps because of their inability to recognise the long term benefits of adult education. Some may say that it is precisely in these matters that voluntary agencies are better placed to show some incentives. Providing immediate cash benefits apart, some sort of benefits like part-time employment, development inputs etc. which some of the agencies are in a position to deliver to the learners in particular, or to their community in general, may not be all that impossible. Probably this was one of the factors that the policy makers had in mind in involving voluntary agencies in the programme. Again it is precisely here that the role of voluntary agencies is underlined. Though the expectation of ecnomic incentive by learners is not entirely wrong the very suggestion points to the somewhat weak motivational techniques adopted by the agencies.

Certain suggestions like starting of adult education centres in separate places like schools are well taken in the sense that there are practical difficulties faced by learners in attending the adult education centre. For instance, a good number of learners reported that during the rainy season they faced many many problems. So also is the suggestion for better lighting facilities.

Such measures like insistence on careful planning, preparation of suitable learning material reflecting the three components well before the starting of the programme, recruitment of competent instructors, therefore demand the attention of the policy agencies.

Certain other suggestions like increasing the functional education component, providing audio and visual equipment to attract and retain the learners are also good which deserve to be taken into consideration. The absence of these minimum necessities will point out the deficiencies of the planning of the programme.

Section V

Drop-outs and Potential learners : their reasons for dropping out and not joining the A E Cs

The socio-economic profile of the dropouts and potential learners has been presented in the first section. In this section an analysis of their reasons for joining the Centre and their reasons for dropping out subsequently will be taken up.

It may be relevant here to mention that the educational planners did not give much importance to the problem of dropouts when the adult education programme was purely voluntary. Several studies conducted on the National Adult Education Programme found it rather difficult to define droputs in a precise way. The problem of dropouts assumes greater significance in view of the need to limit the programme cost and also because of the necessity to cover as many as possible within the stipulated time.

A dropout for the purposes of the present study is defined as he who quits the course before its formal completion.

An analysis of the reasons which contributed to his/her dropping out is considered necessary to appreciate why a particular learner dropped out from the programme. This is intended to help us understand the general attitude of the learners towards the programme. Apart from this, the analysis would throw light on the shortcomings of the programme and provide feedback about it to help the policy makers to carry out necessary modifications in the various aspects of the programme.

However, before we study the reasons for dropouts it must be ascertained as to what reasons prompted him to attend the centre initially. Hence, the schedule on dropouts contains a question on the reasons for joining the programme. It may be mentioned that in the Table 23 dealing with the reasons why learners joined, the dropouts and the potential learners are not included. That is why, the reasons given by those that dropped out need again to be analyzed. The reasons for joining the centre as given by dropouts are presented in the Table 32.

TABLE 32

Reasons for joining A E Cs as stated by dropouts

(in Percentages)

Sl. No.	Reasons for joining A.E.C.	Male	Female
1	To learn general knowledge	21.05	—
2	To learn Alphabet	26.34	42.10
3	To learn reading, writing and numeracy	23.68	26.32
4	Instructors' persuasion	7.89	10.53
5	For higher studies	5.26	—
6	To learn signature	22.63	10.53
7	Group influence	—	10.53
8	Expectation of economic incentives	24.52	20.61
9	To learn about agriculture	7.89	—
10	Leisure time activity	5.26	—

(Percentages do not add up to 100 because of multiple reasons given by respondents)

An analysis of the reasons reveals that about 26.34 percent males and about 42.10 per cent female dropouts cited 'desire to learn alphabet' as their reason for joining the adult education centre. Learning general knowledge as the reason for joining the Adult Education Centre was given by 21.05 per cent of males and 10.53 per cent of female learners.' About twenty three per cent male learners indicated interest in learning how to put their signature as reason for joining the centre. A good number of males (24.52 per cent and females 20.61 per cent) enrolled themselves in the adult education centres with a hope to get some economic incentive. Only 7.89 males in the sample of dropouts joined the adult education centre with a hope to add to their knowledge in agriculture. The reasons for joining like 'for higher studies' and as leisure time activity are cited only by a few (Male and Female) respondents (5 per cent).

It is interesting to observe that about 7.89 male and 10.53 females enrolled themselves at the adult education centres on the persuasion of their instructors. This means that the instructors, in their anxiety to reach the target of 30, persuaded some adults to join the centre. The researcher came across quite a few instances where the instructors approached the illiterates to attend at least for 10 months as they would get some employment.

Thus, as can be seen from the table, the two major reasons for their joining the Centre initially are (a) anticipation of economic incentives and (b) desire to learn the alphabet. There is a strong evidence to believe that some of the agencies did try to attract adults by offering some economic incentives (like offer of loans to those enrolled in adult education centres). However, it could not extend that facility to all those registered. Though there are 'Sangham's (committees) in each village, where a centre was established, the expectation of economic incentive on the part of some learners and their consequent disappointment accounts for a large number of dropouts.

The pattern of attendance of dropouts is investigated with a view to knowing at what point of time a majority of them stopped attending adult education centres. The duration of the programme, as has already been pointed out, is 10 months.

The schedule on dropouts covers the period of the attendance i.e. how many days/months he/she continued to attend the centre. Details of number of months the dropouts attended the centre are given in the following table.

TABLE 33

Attendance of Dropouts

Number of months attended	Male	Female
Less than one month	4(10.53)	—
One month	5(13.16)	5(26.32)
Two months	6(15.79)	7(36.84)
Three months	14(36.84)	4(21.05)
Four months	6(15.79)	3(15.79)
Five months	3(7.89)	—
Total	38(100.00)	19(100.00)

Learners constituting about 36.84 per cent of the total sample dropped out of the Centres after continuing for 3 months. The situation with regard to female learners is more distressing, for as many as seven in the sample (36.84 per cent) dropped out of the course within two months.

Out of thirty eight male learners four (10.53 per cent) dropped out within a month followed by 5(13.16 per cent), and 6(15.79 per cent) for the first and second months. The fourth and fifth mohths of the programme saw another batch of nine male learners (23.68 per cent) withdrawing from the programme.

As far as the female learners are concerned about 26.32 per cent dropped out after 1 month, about 21.05 per cent in the sample dropped out after 3 months, and 15.79 per cent continued to attend for 4 months.

Thus a majority of the learners dropped out when the programme was only half way through. Hence, an investigation into the causes for dropping out is felt necessary. Though, the learners could not precisely identify the type of economic incentives they had in mind, in oral conversation the researcher got the idea that incentives for attending classes (like free food, a daily allowance etc.) as well as incentives in the shape of 'long term' tangible benefits that adult education would confer, were in the minds of the learners. Further, assessing the reasons for dropouts as given by them helps in evaluating the performance of instructors and the officials of the agency.

TABLE 34

Reasons for Dropping out

(in percentages)

Reasons	Male	Female
1. Lack of time	30.53	36.53
2. Employers' lack of co-operation	15.79	—
3. Domestic problems	7.89	26.32
4. Ridicule	5.26	15.77
5. Monotony of teaching	10.53	—
6. Temporarily migrated	10.53	—
7. Unsuitable timings	5.26	10.55
8. Dissatisfaction with teaching	7.89	—
9. Marriage	—	10.53
10. Restricted to teaching alphabet	7.89	15.79
11. Group disinterest	13.17	10.53
12. Functionality component neglected	5.26	—
13. Learned signature	9.42	4.21
14. Learned Alphabet	7.68	3.40
15. Lack of economic incentives	47.45	40.30
16. Bad lighting facility	21.68	20.31

A considerable number of dropouts in the sample (47.45 males and 40.30 per cent females) mentioned lack of economic incentive as the reason for dropping out. If this were to be accepted as valid, it demands the serious attention of the policy makers. This reason cuts across the sex difference as a majority of the female dropouts in the sample too cited it as a cause for dropping out.

A fairly high percentage of female learners (36.53) gave 'lack of time' as the reason for dropping out which is understandable, in the sense that females in rural areas not only work the whole day to earn their livelihood but also have to attend to such invitable domestic chores like looking after children, cooking food for the family etc. About 31 per cent of male learners also, concur that 'lack of time' is the reason for dropping out. The researcher came across many instances wherein the male learners expressed their inability to attend adult education centre due to lack of time as their employers did not allow them to go until late in the night. A good minority of male learners also gave 'non-cooperation' of the employer (15.79 per cent) as the reason for dropping out. Likewise, about 15.79 per cent of the female learners expressed 'fear of ridicule' on account of attending the programme as one of the reasons for dropping out. The researcher also learnt sarcastic remarks being made by others against some of those attending the adult education centres "at this late age."

Bad lighting arrangements forced 21.68 male learners and 20.31 female learners to quit the course. Further,it is interesting to note that a few learners left the course after attaining the ability to sign (9.42 per cent male, 4.21 per cent female). A few female learners (10.53 per cent) discontinued after getting married.

Other reasons also figure in the sample like monotonous teaching (10.53 per cent male), unsuitable timing (5.26 per cent male and 10.53 per cent female), dissatisfaction with teaching (7.89 per cent male), over emphasis on the alphabet (7.89 per cent male and 15.79 per cent female).

Thus, the reasons given by the dropouts reiterates the need for improvements in infrastructural facilities, method of teaching and motivation of learners.

The schedule administered on dropouts also sought to examine the conditions under which they would rejoin the programme.

Table 35 shows that a majority of the respondents in the sample indicated that offering of economic incentive (48.6 per cent male and 4.24 per cent female) is one of the conditions which would make them rejoin an adult education centre. Provision of good lighting facilities is stated by 36.8 per cent male dropouts and 24.4 per cent female dropouts as another important condition for rejoining the centre.

TABLE 35

Conditions for rejoining the centre as stated by dropouts

	Conditions	Male	Female
1,	Flexibility of timing	20.3	30.2
2.	Method of teaching should be changed	7.5	—
3.	More about agriculture should be taught	22.4	11.1
4,	General awareness should be taught	14.1	1.6
5.	Functionality must be included	3.8	1.2
6.	Change in instructor	27.6	—
7.	Good lighting facilities	36.8	24.4
8.	Job facility	22.4	2.4
9.	Economic incentive	48.6	42.4
10.	Separate centre for women	3.8	41.2
11.	No response	10.6	9.0

A good percentage (27.6) of male learners who dropped out expressed a desire to have a change of instructors. A majority among these dropped out from the centres conducted by Durga Sangh Seva Samaj which appointed old and infirm teachers as instructors. A few dropouts (22.4 per cent, 2.4 per cent respectively for male and female) in the sample favoured creation of employment opportunities in the village so that they need not migrate to other villages in search of work.

Flexibility of time (20.3 per cent male and 30.2 per cent female) teaching more about agriculture (22.4 per cent male and 11.1 per cent female) on increasing the topics under general awareness (14.1 per cent male and 1.6 per cent female) are some other conditions put forth by the dropouts for rejoining the centre.

An interesting suggestion to open a separate centre for women (41.2 per cent female and 3.8 per cent male) throws light on the problem both the sexes are confronted within combined centres. Many learners (predominantly female) told the researcher during investigation that they felt shy to attend the centre in the presence of a large number of male learners as that itself inhibited them from learning freely. Instances of male learners making passes at women and making indirect and in some cases direct unseemly suggestions have also been cited by some instructors and learners.

Thus, an analysis of the conditions stated by dropouts point to some of the shortcomings in the implementation of the programme. It must be mentioned here that though such conditions like the economic incentives are difficult to meet immediately other defects that have come to light should be tackled. For example, proper lighting facilities, adequate protection for women participants to come and leave the centre in peace and such other facilities could be provided.

Even in the case of suggestions for economic benefits solutions could be devised. For example, programmes like Integrated Rural Development can be linked to the adult education programme. The possibility of changing the existing methods of identification of beneficiaries under various schemes in Integrated Rural Development programmes need to be explored and adult education centres should be treated as catchment areas for the identification of learners.

Potential Learners

The investigator wanted to find out whether the way in which the agencies went about identifying the learners to join the Adult Education Centres from among the illiterate sections in the village was satisfactory. With this in view he contacted those who did not join the classes to find out the reasons why they did not join. We may choose to call this section of the people as *potential learners*. Here, a small methodological difficulty should be admitted. The adult education programme documents take care to advise that the agencies should identify potential learners from among the vast numbers of illiterates within the age group of 15-35 (i.e. eligible learners) and inform them, and canvass to them about the starting of the centres, and encourage them to join these. Many agencies claimed to have done so. The criteria suggested by the policy makers in identifying potential learners are that they should belong to the age group of 15-35, that they are those who have not had any schooling, and that they show some interest in joining the course. The agencies, as stated earlier, had in fact, approached certain sections of these and from these succeded in making some join the course. But we find that (i) in all centres there were some who did not belong to the age group figure, (ii) that their interest in the courses is less than marginal, and (iii) some of them have had some schooling already. In view of the above, we can conclude that no careful effort was made in identifying the so-called potential learners. The indication is that if only more numbers of the eligible learners (illiterates under the age group) had been more systematically identified, the agencies could have obtained a larger pick from the eligible stream to recruit as learners ; then the need to fill the ceiling of 30 in a centre with some beyond the age group could easily have been avoided.

To highlight this point about the identification of potential learners the investigator himself identified a section of the eligible learners who did not figure among the learners to enquire whether they had been approached if so why they did not join, whether those not contacted would have joined had they been approached and informed about the starting of the centres, and the conditions under which they would have responded positively to the opportunity to join the centres. Thus the category of *potential learners* identified by the researcher is slightly different from the potential learners as stated by the agencies. The following discussion about potential learners based on the responses to the interview schedules administered to them relates to potential learners as identified by the investigator.

As has already been pointed in methodology section of Chapter I two potential learners were selected at random in each of the 19 village where adult education centres are located which comes to 38.

TABLE 36

Potential Learners Identified and Unidentified

Sl. No.	Potential Learners	Male	Female
1.	Identified	13(39.39)	—
2.	Unidentified	20(60.61)	5(100.00)
	Total	33(100.00)	5(100.00)

(Figures in parentheses indicate percentages)

25 potential learners told that they were not contacted by anybody (60.61 per cent male and all the five female learners in the sample) to attend adult education centre. The survey of the agencies is supposed to ascertain not only the age of the potential learners but also his/her interest to join adult education centre as well as his/her educational background. In view of the fact that a good number of the learners fall either above or below the intended age group prescribed by the policy makers and further in view of the fact that a good number, of learners have been exposed to some literacy, it became evident that the survey conducted by the agencies in the sample is not foolproof.

TABLE 37

Reasons for not joining the centre as given by Potential Learners

Sl. No.	Reasons	Male	Female
1.	Domestic Problems	3(9.09)	
2.	Inconvenient timings	4(12.12)	
3.	Fatigue	4(12.12)	
4.	Fear of Ridicule	3(9.09)	
5.	Casteism	3(9.09)	
6.	Not allowed	7(21.21)	4(80.00)
7.	Economic Problems	6(18.19)	1(20.20)
8.	Others	3(9.09)	—
	Total	33(100.00)	5(100.00)

(Figures in parentheses indicate percentages)

Through schedule administered to the potential learners, information was elicited on the reasons for their not joining the adult education centres. Different reasons given by them are given in the above Table 37. Out of the total sample of 38, 33 are male and 5 female respondents. Among these about 7 male respondents (21.21 per cent) and 4 female respondents were not admitted into the adult education centres, as the required number (30) had already been admitted.

eligible learners could not attend due to inconvenient timings. Some other reasons cited by eligible learners for their inability to join adult education centres include 'Fatigue' (12.12 per cent), fear of ridicule (9.09 per cent), casteism (9.09 per cent), reasons like ill health of spouse, ill-health of children, temporary migration and similar reasons are grouped under 'other reasons' which constitute about 9.09 per cent.

As can be seen from the table 'economic problems' and 'inconvenient timings' dominate among the reasons listed by the respondents for their not joining the adult education centres.

The above reasons give us a general opinion of non-learners about adult education programme. The investigator sought the suggestions for making the programme attractive enough to join. The suggestions are given in the Table 38.

TABLE 38

Suggestions for joining the centre as stated by Potential Learners

(in percentage)

Sl. No.	Condition	Male	Female
1.	Change in location of Centre	7.00	40.00
2.	Employers' co-operation	16.40	—
3.	Flexibility in timing	29.00	20.00
4.	Electricity	30.00	20.00
5.	Economic incentives	34.00	15.00
6.	Job facilities	20.00	—
7.	Intensive knowledge about Agriculture	28.20	20.00
8.	Priority in bank loans to learners	25.25	—
9.	Job orientation	15.20	20.00
10.	No conditions	9.09	—

The table indicates that a considerable number of male and female respondents suggested making available economic incentives for attending the programme (34 per cent male and 15 per cent female). This suggestion is closely followed by the need for flexibility in timings of the A E Cs. The investigator attempted to know the reason behind this suggestion. The point is that some of the non-learners tried to make out a case in some villages that they should be allowed to enter adult centre at whatever time they came. Some instructors when contacted turned down the suggestion and told the researcher that it would not in any way help the learner as he could never follow what was taught in adult education centre if he was allowed to enter at any time he chose to attend. Rather they said, the majority opinion in an adult education centre should be allowed to prevail like of a minimum of 15 learners assemble at the centre at the announced time they need not wait for others.

Knowing the difficulties of learning under kerosene lamp, a good section of male (30 per cent) and female (20 per cent) potential learners suggested provision for electric lights in adult education centres.

An interesting suggestion came from about 25.25 per cent of potential learners who wanted priority in bank loans to those who enrolled in adult education centres, which if taken seriously may result in ensuring maximum turn up at adult education centres. A good percentage of potential (15-20 per cent) wanted 'job orientation' to the programme, so that after completion of the course they could find employment on their own. Though this is precisely one of the programme practice so far, it showed no encouraging results. About 29 per cent of males and 20 per cent female learners wanted more information on agriculture for joining in an adalt education centre.

The problems the female 'learners' faced in attending some adult education centres which are located in inconvenient places seems to have prompted a few female learners to demand the change in the location of adult education centres in centres under D S S in Krishna district. (About 40 per cent of the female respondents in the potential learners sample wanted a change in location.) It may be recalled here that a good number of learners dropped out have suggested a separate centre for female learners. The female potential learners in the sample implied the same suggestion. The explanation already given about various problems in combined centres holds good in the case of potential learners also.

Thus the suggestions given by potential learners in the sample for their joining range from offering economic incentives to improvements in course content, infrastructual facilities in adult education centres as well as change in location of adult education centres.

This chapter is divided into five sections: the socio-economic profile of the learners, dropouts and potential learners, the reasons for joining adult education centres, the location of the centres, the reactions of the learners to the material supplied and the reasons for dropping out and views of the potential learners are discussed. The socio-economic profile of the respondents in the sample revealed the agencies have by and large satisfied the objective of attracting the prescribed age group and priority groups like SC, ST and BCs though a careful survey would have ensured entry of more number of eligible learners. The percentage of dropouts underlines the need for use of more effective motivational techniques. Learners responded in a variety of ways to the question on reasons for their joining the adult education centres. More than one reason was cited by them for this question which indicates increasing ability of the rural masses to perceive benefits out of a programme intended for them. On location of adult education centres quite a few respondents preferred pulic places like school, temple etc. which incidentally also brings in a formal class room atmosphere. The respondents also felt that a better lighting arrangement was necessary for sustaining their interests which called for serious attention. A good number reported the receipt of the material like book (s), slate, pencils etc. Of the three components of the programme the agencies gave priority to literacy followed by awareness. As far as functionality is concerned not all agencies have the required infrastructure. Some agencies have also faced problems with regard to implementing awareness component owing to hostile attitude of village elite. On the method of teaching, the agencies have not adopted multi-media approach, instruction is largely confined to face-to-face method. Some learners are also dissatisfied with the method of teaching adopted by some instructors. Various suggestions are made for success of adult education programme. A fairly high percentage of learners suggested linking up the programme with some economic incentive. As for dropouts the reasons cited by them need careful investigation.

Effective survey with the help of a professional research organization by the agencies would have ensured enrolment of eligible learners in some adult education centres. On the whole the programme generated a lot of interest in rural areas. With this we shall go to concluding this study.

NOTES AND REFERENCES

1. See Appendix—
   Interview Schedule III (Learners) ;
   Interview Schedule IV (Dropouts) ; and
   Interview Schedule V (Potential Learners).
2. A learner for the purposes of this study is defined as he who continuously attended the A E C for ten months.
3. A potential learner is one who otherwise is eligible to join A E C as he/she belongs to the prescribed age group, i.e. 15-35, but did not join the Centre for various reasons like not being identified/or did not join for other reasons.
4. A dropout for the purposes of this study is defined as one who attended the Centre for at least *three months* and then discontinued from attending for various reasons.
5. N A E P An Outline : Ministry of Education and Social Welfare, Government of India, New Delhi, 1978, p. 9.
6. Some agencies enrolled learners who are either below or above the prescribed age group which shows partly that the survey supposed to have been conducted by the agencies is not foolproof. The agencies advanced the reason that the identified learner gave them wrong age. However, it is observed that people in rural areas by and large do not exactly remember their age and other details Enrolment of learners above the prescribed age group i.e. 35 led to some problems. Some male learners attended A E C heavily drunk and disturbed the class room atmosphere. The instructor was helpless as it was he who enrolled him. In Centres common to males and females the problems are altogether different. Calling names, use of abusive language also led to friction between two groups of learners. Trooping of children further accentuated

the problem of discipline in some Centres. A more effective survey and a fcw tips to instructors to withstand such exigencies could have resulted in better running of A E Cs.

7. Some women learners expressed reservations about their safety if Centres were located in the instructors' house or other private places.
8. Owing to ill health of some instructors some centres remained closed for months together. The learners blamed the agencies for recruiting such instructors. However, it surprised the investigator to find that the attendance registers spoke about the uninterrupted running of A E Cs.
9. There is variation in both the quantity and quality of reading study material supplied by agencies to the learners. Some agencies have supplied only one book and the quality is fairly satisfactory. Some others supplied more than two books though in quality they were not up to the requirement.

Conclusion

Conclusion chapters are often imprecise as to the nature of their contents. In practice the tasks of sumarisation and recommendation get highlighted together. In this chapter we would first briefly summarise the study as detailed in the preceding chapters and then give some important recommendations relating to the implementation of adult education policy. As the focus of the study is on the role of voluntary agencies, viability of those as the implementors of such a policy is discussed. Recommendations germane to the problem of role of voluntary agencies in such qualitative public policies are also made. To begin with a brief summary of the study is attempted.

In the first chapter the growing importance of the study of Public Policies is discussed. An attempt is made to draw a distinction between policies like adult education and others like prohibition, anti-dowry etc. The policies of latter kind sometimes warrant use of coercion. But as far as policies like adult education are concerned, in a democratic state chances of resorting to coercion are remote and these are realisable only through such techniques like persuasion and motivation. Again, policies like adult education require massive mobilization of human resources. To a great extent thc success of policies like adult education depends on the political will and commitment. A survey of the efforts at educating the illiterate adults before the independence reveals that not much importance was attached to this problem by the colonial government of the day. Only some voluntary agencies and social workers did some work in this direction. Hence, the policy of adult education before independence was one marked by the efforts of the indigenous social workers with a varying degree of success. However, after independence adult education gradually came under public policy agenda. Though financial allocations do not exactly reflect the amount of commitment the Government attach to the adult education policy, it did find a place in the range of policies, the government pursued or attempted to pursue. The success of this policy is sporadic which seems to be not unrelated to the hesitation in commitment of the Government of the day. In addition to the governmental efforts to educate illiterate adults, voluntary agencies which are known for their flexibility in operation, proximity to people and service motto, were also associated with the implementation of this policy. The failure of the official agencies to achieve desired policy objectives also led to search for alternatives, particularly among the non-formal and the non-bureaucratic sector, i.e. voluntary sector, in the implementation of some public policies. It is in this context that some areas of education came to be entrusted to voluntary agencies. This is a study about the role of the voluntary agencies in the implementation of a massive adult education programme.

Studies in education may be regarded as purely the concern of educationists. However, contemporary studies in Public Administration now take under their scope scrutiny themes or areas that were alien in the past to Political Science or Public Administration. Educational policy is a good example. Given the policy and the administrative components that together are intended to achieve the goal of liquidation of illiteracy among adults and the association of non-governmental agencies in the implementation of such policies, the study of such policies offers a challenge to the students of Public Administration also. The specific objectives of this study as mentioned in the chapter include (i) to study and analyse the functioning of the voluntary agencies involved in N A E P (since changed as National Programme of Adult Education) with reference to such administrative aspects as staffing, recruitment and training of instructors and supervisors, problems involved in running adult education centres ; (ii) to study which type of people and with what socio-economic background are attracted to this programme ; (iii) to assess the achievement of learners in terms of the three components, i.e., Literacy, Functionality & Social awareness and (iv) to examine in general, the performance of voluntary agencies.

In the second chapter, the correlation between education and the economic and social development are examined. The data referred to shows that education particularly adult education contributes to rapid social and economic development. A literate population facilitates quickening the tempo of the developmental process. In India, the objective of realising universal primary education by 1960 as envisaged in the Constitution could not be achieved. This and the large increase in population have greatly accentuated the problem of illiteracy and apart from other consequence it seriously hampers development which is vital for the advancement of the country. The UNESCO and other international agencies underlined the need for launching 'campaigns for literacy' to check the growth of illiteracy.

In chapter three, which deals with the Institutional Framework of National Adult Education Programme, the following issues get highlighted.

The Janata Party's coming to power resulted in re-alignment of developmental priorities within education. A high priority had been accorded to adult education. A National Programme to educate about 100 million adult illiterates was launched in 1978. Apart from the Government, the voluntary agencies, Universities, Nehru Yuvak Kendras, are also involved in the implementation of the programme. Thus governmental, semi-governmental and non-governmental agencies are involved in the implementation of the policy of educating adults, between 15-35 age group. A vast administrative machinery was created at the Central, State and District levels. A National Board of Adult Education was established to give higher policy direction and the Prime Minister himself was made the Chairman. At State level, the State Adult Education Boards and Steering Committee are created. The Central Directorate of Adult Education attached to Ministry of Education was expanded and similarly State Directorates of Adult Education were established. These are created for the first time. This in itself is an indication of the high salience given to the programme at this point of time.

The National Board of Adult Education is entrusted with specific functions. Its meetings are not held regularly. In the absence of functioning a regular machinery to give policy direction, ad-hocism can be said to settle, which hampers the realization of the goal. The State Adult Education Boards and Steering Committees are not functioning to the extent the policy framers visualized. It was found that the personnel policy of States with regard to adult education functioning is also marked by ad hocism. A majority of middle level positions are filled by officials on deputation from other conventional administrative departments. Fresh recruitment is confined to Assistant Project Officers and Supervisors' posts. It was found that though it was stated in several documents that voluntary agency should be given precedence in the programme, it was not reflected in spirit. The number of centres run by them is dwindling, the procedures for getting grants are vexatious and the grants are not released in time, with the result reputed voluntary agencies are shying away from participation in the programme. It has also been seen in this chapter how an appraisal of the policy, as befitting a good public policy philosophy was undertaken which candidly held that there had been a noticeable reluctance to give voluntary agencies due encouragement, incentives and autonomy in the running of the programme. Association of students who have gone through or going through formal educational channels as instructors in the programme also remains largely unimplemented.

The fourth chapter deals with the crucial aspects of the instructional cadre of the programme i.e. instructors and supervisors. The qualification recommended and followed in their recruitment, their perceptions and perspective about the programme and relations among themselves are discussed. It has been found that most of the instructors recruited by voluntary agencies belong to the prescribed age group and are fairly educated. The method of recruitment by one of the agencies, BCT in the sample appears to be more rational than followed by others. Though teachers are identified as resource persons it has been found that some retired teachers because of their old age and other problems could not impress the clientele. This suggests the necessity on the part of the agencies to keep in mind the ability of the instructors to teach in centres. Further it has been found that most of the instructors are unhappy with the meagre honorarium.

The method of instruction is dominated by face-to-face teaching. Though the agencies are aware of the advantages of adopting multi-media approach in teaching, lack of facilities is dampening their enthusiasm. It is unfortunate indeed that while we hear reports of non-use of audio-visual equipment on a large scale from one side, from another it is heard that the implementing agencies of Adult Education Programme suffer from the non-availability of such aids. This speaks of the failure of State Directorate of Adult Education in its main function i. e. co-ordination.

One of the important findings of the analysis concerns the quality of the material used for instruction. Different agencies seem to be following different types of instructional material, though those of some agencies here again seem to be much better. However, the question whether instruction material should be standardized and uniform cannot be answered categorically in the affirmative. (That there is a need for diversified material is amply borne out by the fact that learners and instructors in a predominantly dry area are supplied material on wet crops).

The perceptions of the introductors and supervisors on the motivations and enthusiasm of learners is revealing. They report a rather big dropout rate but, at the same time they say that this is due to unavoidable stress that impoverished villagers lay on their economic pursuits. Agencies with diversified economic activities have succeeded more in motivating learners to join as well as continue in adult education centres. As regards the role of village elite, teachers in some centres have to reckon with their resistance to extend educational benefits to the underprivileged. However, in some others, the elite co-operated in a commendable way with the organizers. The role of developmental functionaries is marginal if not insignificant.

It has been observed that most of them view adult education programme like any other programme. While some have avoided any association on the pretext that they are very busy, others disassociated themselves after one or two appearances because of searching questions put by some learners regarding the access to certain economic benefits that would be made available in return for their participation.

The study revealed that most of the supervisors of the sample are young and enthusiastic persons and are fairly educated. That effective supervision also depends on factors such as means of conveyance etc. has also brought out in the study.

As regards co-ordination, the Project Level Committees of the B C T and the CROSS functioned better than others. The procedures followed by these two agencies show that voluntary agencies would also do well to have formal bodies for smooth running of the programme and better achievement of goals. The village level co-ordination committees are mostly dysfunctional.

Coming to the learners and dropouts (ChapterV) a majority of them belong to priority groups like Scheduled Castes, Scheduled Tribes and Backward classes. Thus the policy objective of attracting the intended target group seemed to have been met. A good number of learners recruited, figure above and below the prescribed age group. And in some cases learners with some schooling are also inducted which shows mistakes in the process of identifying learners as prescribed by the policy.

It was found that a majority of learners joined with an intention to acquire three R's. Other reasons like learning to sign, identifying the cinema boards etc. indicate increasing perception of the villagers about the benefits of literacy. It has been observed that the agencies have not succeeded in attracting women learners.

As regards attendance the average daily attendance recorded in A M S and D S S is higher compared to B C T and CROSS. One comment in this connection is necessary. Records like the attendance registers, evidence of use of materials indicate that even in the centresr un by the two latter agencies the performance is rather good. However, from the assessments made by instructors and supervisors and from the views expressed even by the learners, its came out that the performance of the centres which recorded high attendance is lower than average. There is here a clear indication that some agencies speak better than their actual performance.

As regards the achievement of learners it has been found that the trend is not very discouraging. Of three components i.e. Literacy, Functionality and Social Awareness, the Literacy component has been given more emphasis than the other two. Infrastructural and material constraints are cited as some of the reasons for according priority.

As stated earlier the above brief summarisation of the contents of the study was done with a view not merely to high lighting some significant problems relating to the voluntary agencies role in the implementation of National Adult Education Programme. This is also done with a view to suggesting some solutions to the problems identified. While some of these suggestions are implied in the summary itself the following are some major recommendations.

1. The policy on adult education should be accorded high priority considering its significance in national development. The new education policy on cards now spells out the place of adult education in overall educational planning. The increasing pronouncement regarding the use of high technology for national development and the likely emphasis on higher and other sectors of formal education should not be at the expense of non-formal channels, where probably less sophisticated educational technology would be required.

2. The earlier suspicions about the role of voluntary agencies on their alleged political affiliations seemed to have died down which is a good augury. It can be inferred, therefore, that the inhibitions surrounding the credibility of voluntary sector have now receded and the voluntary agencies would be encouraged to participate actively in adult education programme. These is a case for evolving new procedures to attract reputed voluntry agencies. For this the well-established voluntary agencies may be approached for identifying and

orienting the new ones in the implementation of qualitative policies like adult education.

3. As we have noted earlier the National and the State Boards of adult education should be activised and these bodies must meet at least once in a month to take stock of the situation and avoid vacuum in policy making. Further, they are intended to provide a forum for comman identity, exchange of experiences and ideas. By their very composition it is inferred that the formal roles the government i.e. patron and other implementors i.e. clients play are set aside for realization of policy objectives. Thus viewed it appears that the work of these boards goes beyond their formal roles. Hence the N B A E and S B A E's should meet at least once in a month.

4. In terms of financial allocations the adult education policy should not be allowed to suffer. High priority should be given keeping in view the targets and necessary infrastructure should be provided.

Some voluntary organizations are finding it difficult to receive the grants sanctioned to them to run N A E P. It is felt that administrative bottlenecks may be removed and the system may be streamlined to facilitate speedier disposal of grants due to the agencies. A uniform procedure may be evolved to sanction grants and time bound clearance of grants would facilitate quicker decision making.

5. There is an urgent necessity to institutionalise the linkage between adult education and developments. There should be no ambiguity on how the developmental departments can support and reinforce the adult education programme as it exists today. There must be permanent functionaries, or as there should be specific earmarking of functions in the job chart of the developmental functionaries.

6. The voluntary agencies should recruit competent instructors and they should be given proper training. Training instead of a one time affair, possibilities of extending continuing training facilities should be explored.

7. The Supervisors must play more active role in the strengthening of the programme at the field level. Separate provision for vehicles in the project budget should be made for effective supervision.

8. In addition to the National and State resource centres, district level resources centres should be created to strengthen the resource base in order to produce need-based and relevant reading material.

9. The appraisal studies on the impact of N A E P now conducted in some states must be extended to all states and union territories. The voluntary agencies too should conduct appraisals and build up strong information base which can be utilised for heuristic purposes. Feedback affords a good opportunity to correct imperfections, if any, crept into the programme.

19. The project level committees and the village level committees of the voluntary agencies must be activised to facilitate co-ordination. The composition of the Committees must be enlarged with Government representatives, village elite as well as the clientele.

11. The State Directorates of Adult Education must be strengthened with adequate staff especially at the field level. One of the functions of the field personnel should be their active involvement in projects run by voluntary agencies.

12. The personnel policies of the State Government with regard to adult education programme need to be changed. There should be a direct recruitment upto the level of Project Officers or equivalent cadres to attract the best talent. The Central Directorate's Policy in this regard may be recommended to the state. The Union Public Service Commission is entrusted with the responsibility of recruiting Deputy Directors, Assistant Directors' posts. This ensured selection on nationwide basis.

13. The monitoring of the programme also calls for modifications. The achievement of learners in terms of the objectives are not presently reported. Suitable methods may be devised to measure the impact of the programme on the learners.

14. Multi-media approach should be adopted in the instructional strategy to learners. To start with the districts which have literacy percentage below the national average should be given preference in establishing Television and other net-work in order to attract learners and retain them.

15. The voluntary agencies must concentrate more on women illiterates. With regard to women centres the upper ceiling of thirty in enrolment may be relaxed and a package of incentives may be offered to motivate them to attend adult education centres.

BIBLIOGRAPHY

Ahmed, Mushtaq : *Alphabet for Progress* (New Delhi : Indian Adult Education Association) 1970.

Anderson James, E : *Public Policy Making* (New York : Praeger) 1975.

Bhatia, S. C. (ed.) : *Environmental Consciousness and adult education.* (Delhi : University of Delhi) 1980.

Bhatia, S. C. (ed,) : *Some Critical Considerations in adult education* (Delhi : University of Delhi) 1980.

Bhattacharya, Mohit : *Public Administration* (Calcutta : World Press) 1981.

Bordia, Anil et al (ed.) : *Adult Education in India : A book of readings* (Bombay : Nachiketa Publications) 1973.

Budd Hall, L. and Roby, Kidd : *Adult Learning : A design for action* (A Comprehensive International Survey) (Oxford : Pergamon Press) 1978.

Cippola Carlo, M : *Literacy and Development in the West* (London : Penguine) 1967.

Coleman : *Education and Political Development* (New Jersey : Princeton University Press) 1965.

Dewey, John: *Democracy and Education* (New Delhi: Light and Life Publishers) 1976.

Dimock and Dimock : *Public Administration* (New Delhi : Oxford University Press and India Book House Publishers) 1979.

Doraiswami, S : *Curriculum Preparation for adult education programme : An Indian experiment* (New Delhi : Directorate of Adult Education) 1974.

Dutta, S. C. : *New Trends in Adult Education in India* (New Delhi : Indian Adult Education Association) 1962.

Dye, Thomas, R : *Understanding Public Policy* (Prentice Hall Inc.) 1978.

Edwards and Sharskansky : *Policy Predicament : Making and Implementing Public Policy*

Eyestone, Roberts : *The Threads of Public Policy : A Study tn Policy Leadership* (Indianpolis : Bobbs - Merril) 1971.

Freirie, Paulo : *Pedagogy of the Oppressed* (London : Penguine) 1972.

Friedrich, Carl J. : *Man and His Government* (New York : McGraw Hill) 1963.

Hayek : *Road to Serfdom* (London : Routledge and Keganpaul) 1979.

Hobinson, Fredrick and Myers Charles, A : *Education, Manpower and Economic Growth* (New York : Praeger) 1964.

Gandhi, M. K. : *My View on Education* (Gandhi Peace Foundation) 1970.

Gandhi, M. K. : *Constructive Programme* (Ahmedabad : Navjeevan Publications) 1957.

Lall, Dev Indra : *Adulx Education for a new democracy* (Delhi : S. Chand) 1954.

Mathur. J. C. : *Adult Education For Farmers in a developing Society* (New Delhi : Indian Adult Education Association) 1972.

McClelland. D. C and D. G. Winter : *Motivating Economic Achievement* (New York : The Free Press) 1968.

Mohisini, S. R. *Adult and Community Education : An Indian Experiment* (New Delhi : Indian Adult Education Association) 1972.

Naik, J. P. : *Some Perspectives on non-formal education* (Bombay : Allied Publishers) 1977.

Naik, J. P. : *The Education Commission and After* (New Delhi : Allied Publishers) 1982.

Naik, J. P. : *National Education Policy, 1947-78* (New Delhi :

Government of India, Ministry of Education and Culture) 1979.

Ostergaard, Geoffory and Currel Melville : *The Gentle Anarchists* (Oxford : Clarendon Press) 1971.

Rao, T. V., Anil Bhat and Rama Rao T. P. : *Adult Education for Social Change* (New Delhi : Manohar Publications) 1982.

Rao, V. K. R. V. : *Adult Education : A Challenge and an Opportunity* (New Delhi : Ministry of Education and Social Welfare) 1970.

Rao, V. K. R. V. : *Adult Education and National Development* (New Delhi : Ministry of Education and Youth Services) 1970.

Roy, Nikhil Ranjan : *Adult Education in India and Abroad* (New Delhi : S. Chand and Company) 1967.

Shah A. B and Susheela Bhan (ed) : *Non-Formal Education and the N A E P* (Bombay : Oxford University Press) 1980.

Sharma, Atul, Shah Vimal P, Parikh, Bhanumati, K. *Adult Education Programme in Gujarat : An Appraisal* (Ahmedabad : Sardar Patel Institute of Economic and Social Research) 1979.

Schultz, T. W. : *Investing in People* (Delhi : Hindustan Publishing Corpn.) 1980.

Journals

Adiseshaiah, Malcolm S. : "Adult Education & Development", *Asian South Pacific Bureau of Adult Education*, December 1976.

Adiseshaiah, Malcom S : "Some issues posed by non-formal education in India" *Indian Journal of Adult Education*, Vol. No : (39(7).

Aggarwal, I. P. : "Non-formal adult education programme. An aid to rural development", *Education Quarterly*, Vol. No : 31 (1) April 1973.

Ahiuwalla, S.P. & Deouskar, M.D. : "National Adult Education Programme & Integrated rural development", *Indian Journal of Adult Education*, Vol. No. 39 (11-12) Nov./Dec. 1978.

Ansari, N.A. & Rege, K.B. : "Percapita cost of adult literacy in India", *Indian Journal of Adult Education,* Vol. No. : 25 (9), Sept. 1964.

Arrow, K. J.: "Higher Education as a Filter", *Journal of Public Economics,* July 1973.

Baij Nath Singh : Organising a massive programme of adult literacy and adult education", *Indian Journal of Adult Education* Vol. No : 38 (ii), Nov.1977.

Biswas Rajshree : "Changed content : Organisation & Orientation of adult education", *Literacy News,* Vol. No : 5 (3) Sept. 1976.

Chakravarthi, S : "Emerging problems of adult education" *Educational Review,* Vol. No : 69 (ii) Nov. 1963.

Chandrasekharan, Raj Kumari : "Role of voluntary organisation in meeting the needs of women in the fields of adult education and female literacy", *Indian Journal of Adult Education* Vol. No : 38 (5), May 1977.

Chatterjee, Bishwa Bandhu : "Role of adult education in the green revolution", *Indian Journal of Adult Education* Vol. No : 31 (ii), Nov. 1970.

D'Souza, Austin A : "Adult Education in India", *Educator,* Vol. No : 7 (2), April 1953.

Datar, M.K. : "Relevance : the fourth 'R' " *Capital* Vol. No : 182 (4560), June 4, 1979.

Deshpande, A.R. : "Adult Education lost in the woods : Ministry of Education should have total responsibility for adult education", *Indian Journal of Adult Education* Vol. No : 28 (ii), Nov. 1966.

Dharma Vir : "Adult education & Co-operatives", *Indian Journal of Adult Education* Vol. No : 30 (3), March 1969.

Dutta, S.C. : "Role of voluntary organisation in non-formal adult education', *Indian Journal of Adult Education* Vol. No : 39 (7), July 1978.

Eyeford Gun, A : "Role of universities in adult education", *Indian Journal of Adult Education* Vol. No : 29 (4), April 1968.

Fisher Welthy, H : "Each one teach one", *Indian Journal of Adult Education* Vol. No. 16 (2), June 1955.

Freire, Paul : "Are adult literacy programmes neutral" *National Lobour Institute Bulletin* Vol. No : 2 (12), 1976.

Gupta, L.N. : "Linking adult education with life", *Indian Journal of Adult Education* Vol. No : 33 (1), July 1972.

Gupta, N.R. : 'Organisation of adult literacy Programme", *Indian Journal of Adult Education* Vol. No : 29 (4), April 1968.

Gupta, N.R. : "Organisation of adult literacy Progrnmme", *Indian Journal of Adult Education* Vol. No : 29 (4), April 1968.

Jha, V.S. : "Place of adult education in a national Education system", *Indian Journal of Adult Education* Vol. No : 25 (12), Dec. 1964.

Joshi, Uma : "Essential for adult literacy", *Yojana*, Vol. No : 22 (18), Oct. 1, 1978.

Kidd, J.R. : "China Plant and an Indian Cane", Adult learning programmes in India and China". *Indian Journal of Adult Education* Vol. No : 40 (1), Jan. 1979.

Joshi, Vidyut : "Adult education for what" ?, *Economic & Political Weekly*, Vol. No : 16 (1-2), Jan. 3-10., 1981.

Koshy, J.A. : "Voluntary organisations and programmes of adult education", *Indian Journal of Adult Education* Vol. No : 32 (2), Feb. 1979,

Kaul, Lokesh : "Priorities in adult education", *Workers education*, Jan. 1979.

Kumar, S : "Effective utilisation of community resources in adult education", *Indian Journal of Adult Education*, Vol. No : 4 (4), Nov. 1978.

Maitra, S.N. : "Report of the Seminar on the role of voluntary agencies in the National Adult Education Programme", *Indian Journal of Adult Education* Vol. No: 40(1), Jan. 1979.

Mallikarjun, B. : "Role of Radio-newspaper in N E P", *Indian Journal of Adult Education* Vol. No : (3), March 1979.

Mansoor Ahmed : "Income generation projects : the link between adult education andthe satisfaction of basic need", *Indian Journal of Adult Education* Vol. No : 39 (10), October, 1978.

Mathur, J.C. : "Changing concept of adult education", *Indian Journal of Adult Education* Vol. No : 32 (4), April 1971.

Mehta, M.S. : "Adult Education : The meaning & growth", *Naya Shikshak*, Vol No : 8 (2), Oct. 1965.

Mehta, Mohan Sinha : "Concept and Philosophy of adult education", *Indian Journal of Adult Education* Vol. No : 26 (6), June 1965.

Mehta, Prayag : "Dynamics of adult learning and development *Indian Journal of Adult Education* Vol. No : 37 (10), Oct. 1976.

Mohanty, B.B. : "Government's policy statement on adult education—Need to a political will", *Indian Journal of Adult Education* Vol. No: 38 (8-9), Aug/Sept. 1977.

Mukherjee, Pranab : "Eradicating Illiteracy", *Kuruksehtra*, July 1973.

Naik, J.P. : "Adult Education", *Yojana*, Vol. No : 22 (12), July 1, 1978.

Rao, V.K.R.V, : "Adult education in India", *Indian Journal of Adult Education*, Vol. No : 34, Oct—Dec. 1976.

Richard, L.C. : "Role of local bodies in adult education", *Adult Educational Review*, Vol. No : 2 (9), July 1951

Sachdeva, J.L. : "Review of some adult education programmes in India", *Indian Journal of Adult Education*, Vol. No : 25 (10), October 1964.

Schultz, T.W. : "Reflection on Investment in Man", *Journal of Political Economy*, Vol. No. LXX No : 5, part 2, Oct. 1962.

Schwertman, John B : "Adult education : Mean or end "Education" *Indian Journal of Adult Education*, Vol. No. 34 (6), June 1955.

Sharma, B.D. : "National Adult Education Programme and the role of voluntary organisations", *Indian Journal af Adult Education*, Vol: No : 39 (9), Sept. 1978.

Sharma, J.D. : "National Adult Education Programme and the role of voluntary organisation", *Indian Journal of Adult Education*, Sept. 1978.

Sharma, P.C. : "N A E P : The National and regional Objectives", *Journal of Adult Education*, Vol. No : 40(6) June 1979.

Shiviah : "The Political Economy of Universal Literacy in India", *Behavioural Sciences and Community Development*, Vol. No. : 8, No : 2, Sept. 1974.

Singh, T.R. & Bhatnagar, R.C. : "*National Service scheme &*

adult education", *Indian Journal of Adult Education*, Vol. No. 37 (9), Sept. 1976.

Sohan Singh : "Education commisssion and adult education", *Indian Journal of Adult Education*, Vol. No: 27 (88), August 1966.

Sohan Singh : "Historical view of adult education". *Indian Journal of Adult Education*, Vol. No. 29 (5), May 1968.

Subba Rao, D : "New Dimensions to adult literacy", *Social Welfare*, Vol. No : 25 (4), Dec. 1978.

Sundaravadivelu, M.D. : "Administration and organisation in implementing the adult education programme" *Indian Journal of Adult Education*, Vol. No. 28 (2), Feb. 1967.

Veeraraghavan, J. : "Motivation and adult education", *Indian Journal of Adult Education*, April/May 1974.

Venkateshwarlu, B : "Adult Education Programme—Some Lessons", *Mainstream*, Nov. 10, 1979.

Verwayen, Donald : "Comparative philosophies of adult education", *Indian Journal of Adult Education*, Aug. 1973.

William, Harzog, A. Jr. : "Literacy and Community Economic Development in Rural Brazil", *Rural Sociology*, Vol. 38, No. 3, 1973.

Wilson, M. J. & Reddy B.L. : "Attitude of teacher volunteers towards farmers' functional literacy programme : Guntur Study", *Indian Journal of Adult Education*, June 1979.

Yadav, D.P. : "Trends in Indian adult education", *Indian Journal, of Adult Education*, April/May 1974.

Government Publications & Reports

Directorate of Adult Education, (New Delhi), *National Adult Education Programme—Linkages between Adult Education and Other areas of Development*, New Delhi, The Author, 1978.

Directorate of Adult Education (New Delhi), *Training of Instructors : Training of Adult Education Functionaries, No: 3*, New Delhi, Ministry of Education and Social Welfare, 1980.

Directorate of Adult Education (New Delhi). *Methodology of*

Training, No : 2, New Delhi, Ministry of Education and Social Welfare, 1980.

Directorate of Adult Education (New Delhi), *Training of Supervisors : Training of Adult Education Functionaries, No: 3,* New Delhi, Ministry of Education and Social Welfare, 1980.

Directorate of Adult Education (New Delhi), *Monitoring Adult Education Programme,* New Delhi, Ministry of Education and Social Welfare, 1978.

Directorate of Adult Education (New Delhi), *Report on the Working of Farmers Functional Literacy Project in India,* Sept. 1976, New Delhi.

India, Ministry of Education and Social Welfare, *National Adult Education Programme :An Outline.* New Delhi, 1978.

India, Ministry of Education and Social Welfare, *National Adult Education Programme—The First Year,* New Delhi, 1979.

India, Ministry of Education and Social Welfare, *Policy Statement on National Adult Education Programme,* New Delhi, 1978.

India, Ministry of Education and Social Welfare, *National Palicy on Education,* New Delhi, Manager, Government of India Publications, 1969.

India, Ministry of Education and Social Welfare, *Main Schemes of non-formal education,* (in the Fifth Five Year Plan), New Delhi, Manager, Government of India Publications, 1975.

Committee of Members of Parliament on Education (1967), *Report on National Policy on education,* New Delhi, Ministry of Education, 1967.

Committee on Plan Project (Planning Commission). *Report on Social Education.* New Delhi, Planning Commission, 1963.

Committee on Programmes for Women under NAEP (Directorate of Adult Education). *Report.* New Delhi, D A E, 1978.

Committee on Rural Education (Ministry of Education). *Report.* Delhi, Manager of Publications, 1960.

Planning Group on Education (Ministry of Education and Social Welfare). Report on Social education in educational development in Fourth Plan (1969-74). New Delhi, Education Division, 1968.

Report of the Steering Group on Education for the Fifth Five Year Plan, New Delhi : Education Division, Planning Commission, 1973.

Report on the Co-operative movement in Punjab. Punjab : Government of Punjab, 1961.

Report of the Field Study—II, Bagianu Village, Lucknow : Literacy House, 1969.

Motivational Aspect of the N A E P : Interim Report, New Delhi : Ministry of Education and Social Welfare, 1966.

Report of Education Commission, Education and National Development (Chairman, D.S. Kothari) New Delhi : Government of India Publications, 1978.

Summary of the report of the Working Group on Adult Educatlon for Medium Term Plan (1978-83), New Delhi : Ministry of Education and Social Welfare, 1978.

Seminar papers and proceedings of the UNESCO contribution to the "World Programme with Reference to India", *Eradication of Illiteracy*, New Delhi : Council for Social Development, 1970.

Review Committee Report on National Adult Education Programme : Ministry of Education and Social Welfare, New Delhi. Manager, Government of India Publications, 1980.

Unpublished Ph. D. Theses

Agnihotri, "Evaluation of the Programme of Adult Education in operation under Pilot Plan in Wardha District", (Ph. D. Thesis, Unpublished) 1974, Nagpur University, Nagpur.

Khan, M.Z, The Problem of Social (Adult) Education in four districts of Bombay and Mysore, Dharwar (Unpublished Ph. D. thesis) 1958, Karnataka, Dharwar.

Johnson, J.P. "A proposal for the Establishment of a Statewide Adult Education Programme for Tamil Nadu (Ph. D. thesis, Unpublished), Madras University, Madras, 1970.

Newspapers

Andhra Patrika (Telugu daily), Hyderabad.
Andhra Prabha (Telugu Daily), Hyderabad.
Deccan Chronicle, Hyderabad.
Eenadu (Telugu daily), Hyderabad.
Indian Express, Hyderabad.
Statesman, New Delhi.
The Hindu, Hyderabad.
Times of India, Bombay.

Appendix

Interview Schedule —I
Instructor

Background information of the respondents :

1. Name of the respondent :
2. Address :
3. Father's/Husband's name :
4. Age of the respondent :
   (Actual age——)
5. Sex : 1. Male 2. Female
6. Educational Status : (Actual qualifications)
   (0) Illiterate
   (1) Literate
   (2) Primary
   (3) Secondary
   (4) Intermediate
   (5) Collegiate/Univ.
   (6) Vocational/Technical
   (7) Any other specify.
7. Caste : (Name——)
   (1) Scheduled Caste
   (2) Scheduled Tribe
   (3) Backward Caste
   (4) Other Castes.
8. Marital Status :
   (1) Married
   (2) Unmarried
   (3) Widowed
   (4) Divorced.

8. 1. Family particulars :

Sl. No.	Category	Number of Males	Number of Females	Total
1.	Children (0-14)			
2.	Adults (15-49)			
3,	Old (60 and above)			

9. Economic Status :
Income per month
(Actual amount : Rs.——)

9. 1. Do you own or have any share in any immovable property :
1. Yes 2. No 3. ONE

9. 2. What is its present value ?
1. Residential : Rs.——
2. Landed : Rs.——
3. Others : Rs.——

10. Occupational Status :
1. Agricultural Labourer
2. Small Farmer
3. Educated Unemployed
4. Teacher (retired or in service specify)
5. Employee of the local Temple, Church, Mosque
6. Any other specify——

11. How did you come to know about the adult education programme ?
1. Member of the Voluntary Agency :
2. Media (Radio, Newpaper & T. V)
3. Officials of the voluntary agencies approached.
4. Any other specify——

12. Do you have any experience in teaching Adults ?
    1. Yes 2. No
    If yes, please specify the nature of experience with details.

13. SELECTION, RECRUITMENT :

    Did you apply for the post of Instructor or were you approached by the Agency.
    1. Applied
    2. Approached by the Agency
    3. Any other.

13.1. What is the method of selection ?
    1. Written Test
    2. Interview
    3. Written Test and Interview
    4. Personal contact
    5. Any other method specify——

13.2. What is the composition of the Selection Committee?
    1. Officials of Agency only
    2. Officials of the Govt. and Agency
    3. Officials of the University & Agency
    4. Any other.

13.3. What type of questions were asked in the written/oral test ?
    1. Written Test
    2. Oral Test :

14. TRAINING :

14.1. Did you undergo any training ?
    1. Yes 2. No
    If yes, please give the following details ;

Phases of training	Place of training	Content of training	Period
1			
2			

14.2. What was the main emphasis of training ?

14.3. What were the other aspects of the training ?

14.4. What do you feel about training programme ?

1. Extremely useful
2. Adequate
3. Irrelevant to adult education programme.
4. Any other specify.

14.5. What material was supplied to you as part of training ?

14.6. What do you feel about the material supplied to you?

Identification of Learners :

15. Were you associated with the process of identification of learners :

1. Yes 2. No.

If yes, what methods have you adopted to identify learners.

1. Survey of all houses
2. Based on Census data
3. Based on block plans prepared by the State Govt.
4. All the above
5. Any other.

15.1. If the identification is through survey method what aspects did the survey contain.

1. Age
2. Interest
3. Any other.

16. How did you recruit learner after identification ?

17. What were the problems in the identification of learners ?

18. **Awareness about** N A E P ?

What are the objectives of N A E P

18.1 What should be the objectives of N A E P ?

19. **Opinion on Components of the Programme** :

What are the main components of the programme ?

19.1. What in your opinion should be weightage given to three main components (Literacy, Functionality and Social Awareness) ?

Sl. No.	Name of the Component	Weightage (or) Priority Higher	Adequate	Low	Judicious combination of all
1.	Literacy				
2.	Functionality				
3.	Social Awareness				

19.2. What topics have you covered under :
1. Functionality
2. Social Awareness.

DROPOUT

20. How many learners in your Centre completed the course?

20.1. How many dropped out ?

20.2. What do you think were the reasons for their dropping out ?

1. Economic reasons
2. Course not interesting
3. Harvest Season
4. Any other.

20.3. What are your suggestions for controlling the problem of dropouts.

21. **Opinion on Te aching, Resource Material :**

Have you received the teaching/learning material in time?
1. Yes 2. No.

21.1. Did you get them in sufficient number?
1. Yes 2. No.

21.2. How far are these related to the learner's occupation.

21.3. Have you prepared any charts/posters or any other teaching/learning.

22. **Support and Co-operation :**

Sl. No.	Category	Yes	No	Satisfactory	Unsatisfactory	Poor
1.	Supervisor					
2.	Project Officer					
3.	Local leaders					
4.	Govt's Officials					
5.	Learners.					

23. **Opinion on Supervisor**

Did the Supervisor visit your Centre in course of the Programme?
1. Yes 1. No

23.1. If yes, how many times did he visit your Centre ?
No :———

23.2. What in your opinion was the nature of his visit-
1. Fact—finding
2. Fault—finding.

23.3. What type of guidance was provided by him.

24. Did you visit any other Adult Education Centre run by colleagues in your agency or any other agencies?
1. Yes 2. No.

24.1. If yes, what were your experience.

25. Do you think it would be better to rotate instructors once in a month through all centres under the agency.
1. Yes 2. No.
If yes, what are the advantages of this move.

26. **JOB SATISFACTION**

Are you satisfied with your job?
1. Yes 2. No.

26.1. Have you received your salary regularly ?
1. Yes 2. No.
If no, what were the reasons.

26.2. Are you satisfied with the salary?
1. Yes 2. No.

26.3. Do you wish to work again as instructor?
1. Yes 2. No.
If yes, where (1) in the same Centre
(2) Change needed
(3) Any particular choice specify——

26.4. Did you ever think of quitting the job in course of the programme.
1. Yes 2. No.
If yes, why did you want to quit ?
1. Not interested in teaching
2. Conditions of work not encouraging
3. Salary not attractive
4. Authoritarian attitude of the head of the Organization
5. Any other.

Suggestions :

27. Would you describe briefly the functioning of the Centre in general and the attitude of the learners.

28. What type of change did you expect in the adults and

what type of change did you notice after the completion of the cou.se.

29. What were the follow-up (post-literacy) programmes contemplated by your Agency.

30. Do you have a Library in your village
    1. Yes 2. No.

31. Do you think establishment of Library helps to strengthen the post-literacy programme.
    1. Yes 2. No.

32. How far mass media (Radio, T.V., Newspaper) helps in retaining the knowledge acquired by adults.

33. How should an adult education programme be devised in your opinion for the development.
    1. Knowledge
    2. Skills
    3. Attitudes.

34. Would you like to offer any suggestions for the effective implementation of the programme.

Interview Schedule-II

Supervisors

Personal Particulars

1. Name of the respondent :
2. Address :
   Father's/Husband's name :
   Father's/Husband's occupation :
2. Age :
   (Actual age——)
   1. 15-35 years
   2. 36-59 years
   3. 60 years and above
3. Sex : 1. Male 2. Female
4. Educational Status
   (0) Illiterate
   (1) Literate
   (2) Primary
   (3) Secondary
   (4) Vocational/Technical
   (5) College/University
   (6) Any other specify.
5. Caste
   (Name :——)
   (1) Scheduled Caste
   (2) Scheduled Tribe
   (3) Backward Caste
   (4) Other Castes.

6. Marital Status :
   (1) Married
   (2) Unmarried
   (3) Widowed
   (4) Divorced
   ONR

7. Family particulars :

Sl. No.	Number of Males	Number of Females	Total
1. Children 0-14 years			
2. Adults (15-59 years)			
3. Old (60 years and above)			
Total			

8. Economic Status :

   (Income per month :

   Actual amount———)

9. Occupational background :

   What positions have you held before joining this organization.

No.	Positions held	Nature of work	Salary/Honorarium if any

10. When did you join in this Organization ?

11. Why did you join in this Organization ?

12. Why did you take up this position as Supervisor?

13. Do you have any special interest in Adult Education?

    1. Yes   2. No

If yes, can you briefly tell your previous experience.

14. Have you worked as Instructor/Organizer of any educational programme?

    1. Yes 2. No

15. When did you come to know about National Adult Education Programme?

    1. 1977
    2. 1978
    3. 1979
    4. 1980

16. How did you come to know about National Adult Education Programme.

    1. Newspapers
    2. Working in the Agency since a long time
    3. Approached by the officials of the Agency
    4. Deputed by the Government to supervise adult education programme
    5. Any other specify.

OBJECTIVES :

17. What are the objectives of the N A E P

18. What in your opinion should be the objectives of NAEP

Awareness about the agencies involved in N A E P :

19. What are the other agencies involved in implementation of N A E P

    1.
    2.
    3.
    4.

Selection, Recruitment and Training :

20. Did you yourself apply for this post ?

    1. Yes 2. No

    If no, who asked you to apply for the post ?

21. What is the method of selection ?
    1. Written Test
    2. Oral Test
    3. Written and Oral
    4. Appointment by personal contact
    5. Any other.

22. Did you unndergo training ?
    1. Yes 2. No
    If yes, particulars of training.

Phases	Places of training	Sponsored by	Organized by	Contents	Period
1					
2					

23. What do you feel about the material supplied to you as part time programme.

24. Do your think the material supplied to you as part of training is relevant to you.
    1, Yes 2. No

25. What are you suggestions for improving the training programmes.

Target Achievement :

26. What was the target fixed for this programme in your agency (Target in terms of adult learners and Centres)

27. To what extent this target had been achieved.

28. If the target has not been achieved what were the problems in achieving it.

Method of Supervision :

29. Can you tell me what are the functions of a Supervisor as envisaged by N A E P ?

(1) Assisting the Project Officer in resource development and particularly in training of instructors.
(2) Checking attendance and initiating measures to combat drop-out problem.
(3) Discussions with instructor, guiding them on the methods of teaching.
(4) Keeping up the morale of the instructor.
(5) Maintenance of regularity of classes.
(6) Taking steps to achieve targets.
(7) Meeting learners to get feed back about the instructor.
(8) Liaison with the local development functionaries extension officers.

30. What are effective supervisory techniques.
(1)
(2)
(3)
(4)
(5)

31. Are you able to use them.
1. Yes 2. No
If no, what were the reasons.

32. How many centres have been put under your supervision
No :-——

33. How many times have you inspected them in a month/week.

34. How many surprise inspections have you undertaken.

35. Did you find the functioning of Centres as
1. Very satisfactory
2. Satisfactory
3. Not satisfactory
4. Any other.

36. How did you resolve the difficulties faced by you.
1. Consulting Project Officer

2. Office-bearers of the Organization
3. Govt. officials
4. Any other.

37. How did you check the absence of the instructor.
    1. By issuing warning
    2. Reprimanding orally
    3. Termination
    4. Condoning the mistakes
    5. Any other.

38. What type of instructors are attracted to this Programme ?

39. Can you suggest any method for attracting better instructors?

Resource Material :

40. How far do you think the resource material is relevant to the local needs and requirements of the people.

41. What improvements do you suggest with regard to the supply of resource material and changes in the contents.

Opinion on linkage with other developmental programmes in the area :

42. One of the objectives of the N A E P is to link it with other rural developmental programmes. Can you tell me whether you have tried to link the A E P with other developmental programmes.
    1. Yes 2. No
    If yes, please give me some details.

42.1. If no, why did you not attempt to establish link.

43. **Reporting Monitoring** :

    How did you record the progress of the Programme :
    1. Prepared proforma of the Government

2. Proforma prepared by the Agency
3. Any other.

43.1. Have you received the following reports from the instructors in time ?

1. Instructors initial report 1. Yes 2. No
2. Instructors Monthly report 1. Yes 2. No

44. What aspects of the programmes did you discuss in monthly meetings with Project Officer and instructor :

1
2
3

45. What modifications have you affected after getting these reports in the administration of the programme.

46. Are you satisfied with the reporting monitoring mechanisms of the programme :

1. Yes 2. No

If no, what changes do you contemplate.

47. Do you think the reporting procedures prescribed by the Government are too rigid and time consuming.

1. Yes 2. No

If yes, did you comply with them only because there is no alternative ?

1. Yes 2. No

Opinion on Learners :

48. What in your opinion is the reaction of the learners to the programme?

49. What steps have you taken to sustain their interest ?

EVALUATION:

50. If some A E C's are running successfully what were the reasons.

51. If some A E C's are not running successfully what were the reasons.

52. What are your general impressions about the progress of the Programme.

53. Basing on your experience, do you think this programme would become effective in course of time.

54. Did you ever think of quitting the job in course of the programme.

    1. Yes 2. No

    If yes, why did you want to quit.

    1. Adult Education work not interesting.
    2. Conditions of work not encouraging.
    3. Not satisfied with the progress.
    4. Salary is not commensurate with responsibility.
    5. Authoritarian attitude of the Project Officer/other Office-bearers.

55. What are your suggestions for effective implementations of the Programme.

Interview Schedule—III

Learners

1. Name :
2. Father's/Husband's Name ;
3. (a) Female (b) Male
4. Age : (a) 5-14 years
   (b) 15-35 years
   (c) 36-59 years
   (d) 60 years and above
5. Caste/tribe : (a) Scheduled Caste
   (b) Scheduled Tribe
   (c) Backward Class
   (d) Other caste.
6. Occupation : (a) Small farmers
   (b) Marginal farmers
   (c) Agricultural Labourers
   (d) Govt. employee
   (e) Private employee
   (f) Village Artisan
   (g) Others.

7. Income Status (Per Annum) : (a) Below 500
   (b) Rs. 501-1500
   (c) Rs. 1501-2500
   (d) Rs. 2501-3500
   (e) Rs. 3501-4500
   (f) Rs. 4501-5500
   (g) Rs. 5501 and above
8. Property : (a) Landless labourers/ owner of land
   (i) from 0.01 to 2.49 acres
   (ii) from 2.5 to 4.49 acres.
   (iii) from 5 to 9.99 acres
   (iv) 10 acres and above.
9. Do you own a house ? (a) Yes (b) No
   (i) Thatched (ii) Katcha
   (iii) Asbestos (iv) Others
10. Marital Status :
    Are you married ? (a) Yes (b) No
    If yes, number of children : Boys——
    Girls——
11. Educational Qualifications :
    (i) Illiterate (ii) Literate (iii) 1, 2, 3, 4, 5, 6, classes and above
12. Do you have a school in your native village ?
    1. Yes 2. No
    If yes, did you attend it or have you studied privately or have you attended school in another village.
13. To what class was the instruction offered.
14. Up to what class have you studied in that school ?
15. Reasons for discontinuing the education :
    (i) Economic reasons

(ii) Inadequate teaching
(iii) Not permitted by the elders
(iv) Education is devoid of purpose
(v) Other reasons, if any.

16. Reasons for not attending the School.
(a) Lack of a school in village
(b) Distance
(c) Refused admission by teachers
(d) Financial reasons
(e) Discouraged by family members
(f) Other reasons, if any.

17. Parents'/Grand parents' educational level :
Did your parents/Grand parents attend a school
(a) Yes (b) No
If yes, up to which class did they study
(a) Grandfather/Grandmother
(b) Father/Mother.

18. How did you come to know about Adult Education Programme
(a) Friends
(b) Organizers
(c) Mass Media (Radio, T.V., Newspapers)
(d) Voluntary Agencies/Govt. Agencies
(e) Village elders
(f) Other sources if any.

19. Opinion on Adult Education :
Advantages of Adult Education.
(a)
(b)
(c)

20. Has anybody informed you about those advantages
(a) Yes (b) No

21. Literary Status ;

Do you know how to write Telugu alphabet ?

22. Can you read the following numbers.

1	2	3	4	5	6	7	8	9	10
12	14	19	100	150	350	1000			

23. Can you solve the following arithmetical problems ?

If 8 is added to 6	If 5 is added to 18
If 120 is subtracted from 200	If 8 is subtracted from
50×100 : 5×2 :	If 9 is divided by 3.

24. Have you been told about the following occupation in Adult Education Centres.

(a) Carpentry (b) Pottery (1) Agriculture
(2) Weather
(3) Chemical Fertilizers
(4) High Yielding varieties
(5) Income increasing activities (for e.g. co-ordinating)
(6) Use of occupational instruments
(7) Agricultural mechanisation.

25. Have you benefited by attending adult education centre ? Social Awareness.

26. Have the organisers told you about the following issues ?

Sl. No	Issue	Yes	No	Remark
1	Our village			
2	Panchayat Raj			
3	Nutritious food			
4	Animal Husbandry			
5	Health (cleanliness)			
6	Minimum wage of Agricultural Labourers			
7	Democracy			
8	Family Planning			
9	National Integration			
10	Any other issues			

27 What is your opinion on the following issues
   (a) Causes of Poverty
   (b) Govt. developmental schemes, help extended to the poor people
   (c) Superstitions
   (d) Banks and other co-operative agencies.
   (e) Equal opportunities
   (f) Opinion of the village elders about your Education.

Learning timings :

28. Did you have classes every night : (a) Yes (b) No

29. Are you attending the Centre regularly : (a) Yes (b) No

30. What are the timings : From——to——

31. Are these convenient (a) Yes (b) No
    If no what timings suit ? From——to——

32. Did you receive the following ?
    (a) Slate (b) Slate pencil (c) Books (d) Others.

Lighting facilities :

33. Is your village electrified ? (a) Yes (b) No

34. Has your centre got electric connection ?
    (a) Yes (b) No
    If not how did you mange ?
    (a) Petromax Light (gas light)
    (b) Oil lamp
    (c) Hurricane Lamp
    (d) Others, if any.

35. Have you used Lamps. Are they convenient :
    (a) Yes (b) No
    If not, state reasons.

Motivational Aspects :

36. Have your family members encouraged you to join the adult education centre (a) Yes (b) No.

37. Have your friends encouraged ?
(a) Yes (b) No

38. Has anyone told you not to attend the Centre ?
Yes No

If yes, (a) Who told you
(b) Why did they tell you
(c) What was your reply ?

Opinion on your Supervisor :

39. What is your opinion of your supervisor.

40. Is he/she teaching sincerely (a) Yes (b) No
If not, what do you think are the reasons :
1
2
3

41. Did the instructor attend regularly
(a) Yes (b) No

42. Have you got your doubts cleared from your instructor
(a) Yes (b) No
If yes, usually what are the issues you have asked your instructor
1
2
3

43. Has he solved your doubts to your satisfaction ?

44. In your opinion what are the good qualities of an instructor
1
2
3

45. Do you know your supervisor's name ? (a) Yes (b) No
If known, can you tell me

46. Have you met your supervisor anytime during the course ?
(a) Yes (b) No

47. How many times he/she used to come to your centre in a week ?
1 2 3 Don't know.

48. Have you realised the usefulness of education now ?
(a) Yes (b) No
If yes, will you send your children to the school?
(a) Yes (b) No
If not, will you give the reasons ?

49. Will you tell your friends to attend the adult education centres ?
(a) Yes (b) No
If not, can you explain the reasons
1
2
3

50. What are your suggestions for the success of an adult education programme ?

Interview Schedule—IV

Dropouts

1. Name :
2. Age :
3. Occupation :
4. Annual income :
5. Have you attended School ? :
6. Why did you join A E C ? :
7. For how long have you attended ? :
8. Why did you dropout ? :
9. Would you like to join again ? :
10. If yes, under what conditions ? :
11. What are your suggestions for better organisation of Adult Education Centre :

Interview Schedule—V

Potential Learners

1. Name of the Centre/Village :
2. Name of the respondent :
3. Sex : 1. Male 2. Female
4. Age :
5. Caste :
6. Occupation :
7. Marital Status :
8. Annual Income :
9. Literary level : (1) Grand Father
   (2) Father
   (3) Respondent
10. Location of the house from the Centre :
11. Did you know about the Adult Education Centre in the village : (1) Instructor
   (2) Teaching
12. Did you talk with any of the :

13. If yes, in what context and what was her/his impression :

14. Were you identified as learner by the instrctor or any body : (1) Yes (2) No.

15. What are the reasons for not joining the Centre :

16. Would you like to attend the Centre now ? :

17. If yes, under what circumstances :

Interview Schedule—IV

Village Level General Observation Schedule

This schedule is being employed for understanding the general profile of the vi llage in relation to its income groups, resources available in th e villages, occupational structure. The information that is being collected may throw light on the nature of curriculum that could be developed for people of that area/region. The material for the second component of the programme i.e. Functionality could be gathered through this schedule. The sources of collecting data are discussions with number of people and general observation of the village.

1. Village profile :

   Details regarding :
   (1) Minerals
   (2) Agriculture crops
   (3) Type of land
   (4) School, year of starting the school. If there is no School (nearest school)
   (5) Hospital
   (6) Water Supply
   (7) Irrigation facilities
   (8) Any other specify.

2. Caste structure :
   1. Whether the village has single caste group

2. Multi caste group
3. Dominant caste.

3. Political learning in general.

4. Transportation facilities
(Approachability, Mobility of the people)

5. Distance in KMs from the nearest town.

6. Occupation : Main Occupation.

   1

   2

   3

   4

   5

7. Exposure to mass-media
(The presence and/use of the mass media to be recorded)

8. Government Agencies in/around village.

9. Industries/Factories in proximity of the village.

10. Some major characteristics of the village and surrounding areas, e.g. : Forest, Hills, Mines, any special occupation.

Interview Schedule—VII

Centre Level Data Schedule

This schedule is intended for getting details regarding the Organizational aspects of the adult education centres. Issues like the location, attendance, physical facilities, supply of materials, help received from the villagers would be studied. Records maintained at the Centre by the Instructor would be consulted and verifications will be made.

1. Name of the Centre and Village

   (Code No : if any———)

2. Name of the Instructor :

   (Details of previous instructors if any)

3. Location of the Centre : 1. Open Space
   2. House
   3. Public building
   4. Any other specify.

4. Facilities : 1. Lighting
   2. Space
   3. Any other specify.

5. Whether the Centre is nearer to where elite group are living or at the periphery nearer to some of the low socio-economic groups are living—details.

6. Date of starting of the Centre :
7. Total number enrolled :
8. Max. attendance :
9. Min. attendance :
10. Number of dropouts :
11. Average attendance :
12. Total number of days the Centre was run :
13. Equipment available in the Centre :
14. Supply of material to learners :
15. Help received from the village.

APPENDIX

Agency	*Name of Village/Adult Education Centre*
Andhra Mahila Sabha	Namapur
(A M S)	Pachammavadi (W)
	Avunoor
	Gambhiraopet
	Tadoor
	Namapoor (W)
	Gandalipur
	Tangallapalle
	Pannalur
	Gapalraopalle
Bhagavathula Charitable	Murakada
Trust (B C T)	Mamidivada
	Dharapalem
Comprehensive Rural	Gudur
Operations Service Society	Wanganpally
(C R O S S)	Vartoor
Durga Samaj Seva Sangh	Dawajeeguden
(D S S)	Akunuru
	Ogirale